The
PRAYER
of MARY

LIVING *the* SURRENDERED LIFE

KEITH A. FOURNIER
with LELA GILBERT

OLIVER
NELSON

NELSON BOOKS
A Division of Thomas Nelson Publishers
Since 1798

www.thomasnelson.com

Published in Nashville, Tennessee, by Thomas Nelson, Inc.

Library of Congress Cataloging-in-Publication Data

Fournier, Keith A., 1954–
  The prayer of Mary : living the surrendered life / Keith Fournier with Lela Gilbert.
    p. cm.
  ISBN 0-7852-1173-X (pbk.)
  1. Mary, Blessed Virgin, Saint—Meditations. 2. Spiritual life—Catholic Church.
I. Gilbert, Lela. II. Title.
  BT608.5.F68 2005
  232.91—dc22   2004030760

Printed in the United States of America
1 2 3 4 5 6 RRD 08 07 06 05

Words of Praise for *The Prayer of Mary* . . .

"*The Prayer of Mary* presents the *Fiat* of Mary as a model for all genuine prayer and Mary's devotion to her Son and Savior as the path for all Christians. I believe this book will change the hearts, minds, lives and lifestyles of many, leading them to a deeper walk with God. In an age that seems to have lost its heart, Deacon Keith Fournier's beautifully written book reintroduces the world to the woman who we still call 'Blessed' and the way that leads to true freedom and peace."

—Senator Rick Santorum
United States Senator, Pennsylvania

"John Paul the II's greatest wish during his pontificate, echoing the Gospel, was that 'that all might be one.' It was the most important goal that he did not reach during his graced life. Deacon Keith Fournier, a man of the 'New Evangelization' in so many aspects, has written a book on Mary, the mother of God, whom he clearly sees as the person who can bring all Christians together so that we worship the Lord as one. Only through imitating Mary the Virgin in her prayer, humility, and deep personal love of the person of Jesus will we achieve that goal for the glory of God and the good of the whole world. Few men in our time have labored more diligently for true ecumenism than Keith Fournier. This book marks another important stage in uniting us so that we can more effectively preach and live the Gospel of Life to our society as Mary lived it out in her own life."

—Fr. C. John McCloskey III
Catholic Priest of the Prelature of Opus Dei
Research Fellow, Faith and Reason Institute

"Deacon Keith A. Fournier is a gift to the Church in our time. His writings, beyond 'left' and 'right' factionalism, reflect a depth of spiritual and analytical insight which is a signpost for the New Evangelization already underway."

—Stephen Hand
Author, Editor, TCRNews.com

"Do you have a love for the Blessed Virgin Mary? Here is a book to help you delve wonderfully, Biblically, and historically into her heart and her role in salvation history. Are you among those who wonder what all the fuss is about? Here is a book to give you a panoramic view of this incredible woman used mightily of God whom you will soon grow to love. Deacon Keith Fournier has so captured the heartbeat of the woman the Church has called the 'Theotokos' (the Mother of God) for two thousand years, that his words will transcend East vs. West, Protestant vs. Catholic, and Historic vs. Modern. I not only recommend this book, I will be giving them away."

—RANDOLPH SLY
Archbishop, Eastern Province
Supervising Archbishop for the Office of Communications
The International Communion of the Charismatic Episcopal Church

"Keith Fournier has given a great gift to the whole body of Christ by showing us that Mary's obedience and spirituality are models for our own relationships with Jesus. Of all the personalities in the story of the Gospel, few figures are as large as Mary. Sadly, we Protestant Evangelicals have virtually ignored her. Yet, Mary was the first to 'accept Jesus' when she said yes to the angel, and she remained closer to our Lord than any person on earth. This is an excellent, tender and beautifully written study of the most important mother—some might say the most important Christian—who ever lived."

—REV. ROB SCHENCK, D.D.
Past board member, Evangelical Church Alliance
President, National Clergy Council, Washington, DC

"*The Prayer of Mary* introduces contemporary readers to Mary, the Mother of Jesus, as a model and mother for all Christians. We Eastern Christians cherish her as 'Theotokos,' the Mother of God and Christ Bearer. Our Byzantine 'Hymn of Praise' called the 'Akathist in Honor of our Lady Theotokos' (Mother of God) expresses, in poetic and devotional verses, the beauty of the Woman whom all generations call blessed. In every Liturgy she is given her place of honor—as she should in the prayer and lifestyle of every Christian. As this beautiful book so clearly explains, Mary inspires us, through her words and witness, to lead a life fully surrendered to God. *The Prayer of Mary* is a treasure. It inspires its readers to find their place at the Cross of Jesus Christ, where God's Mercy is manifested for the whole world. There we join His Mother and our Mother, in Prayer. Deacon Fournier is a friend whose work has helped to bridge the gap that has unfortunately separated too many Christians for far too long. *The Prayer of Mary* will continue his important work by bringing many into a deeper relationship with God. I recommend it highly."

—BISHOP JOHN ADEL ELYA, B.S.O.
Eparch Emeritus of the Diocese of Newton, Byzantine Catholic Bishop
Melkite Greek Catholic Eparchy of the United States

CONTENTS

CONTENTS

PART THREE: MARY'S WAY

Just as Eve, wife of Adam, yet still a virgin, became by her disobedience the cause of death for herself and the whole human race, so Mary too, espoused yet a virgin, became by her obedience, the cause of salvation of both herself and the whole human race.

—St. Irenaeus of Lyons, Against Heresies, III, 22

PREFACE

Several years ago my wife and I were invited to celebrate the life of Pat Robertson, the well-known evangelical leader. We were guests at a black tie affair, which was held in a posh ballroom in Southern California. It was a wonderful experience for us to participate in an event that paid tribute to a man who had had an influence on my own unusual life and career. The crowd, however, was not one in which we would normally feel comfortable. We were among only a handful of Catholic Christians who attended the gathering.

Most of the evening was filled with accolades, stellar musical performances, and multi-media presentations honoring this high-profile Protestant leader. It was a birthday celebration, filled with laughter, lighthearted reflections, and the consumption of the finest of fare. Finally, at the end of the evening, Jack Hayford, beloved pastor of the Church on the Way, gave a concluding address and prayer to sum up the night's festivities and to send all the participants away to make a difference in the world.

I was truly surprised by the way he ended his comments. It was better than any of the food courses because it satisfied a deeper human hunger, a hole in the soul. Pastor Hayford's message (to the surprise of some) was that we are living in what he called a "Mary Moment." With genuine affection and deep insight, he broke open the meaning of the life and mission of

Mary, the mother of our Lord. He held her up as a model for every person in that room who would follow her Son into the third Christian millennium.

I was delighted with his words. Afterward, I began to think more specifically about what Mary says to each of us.

In the New Testament texts we find very few words spoken by Mary, but there is no lack of her presence at the most significant events in the life, ministry, death, and resurrection of Jesus Christ, and therefore in the great events of salvation history. Mary encountered God in profound ways from the beginning to the end of her life.

During the earthly life of God's Son, His every word and every act was redemptive, revealing the presence of God, the mystery of heaven touching earth, and the deeper purpose of our own lives when lived entirely for Him.

Mary was present at the incarnation, birth, crucifixion, and resurrection of the One whom Christians proclaim as God Incarnate. She was there throughout the so-called hidden years, during His life at Nazareth where ordinary work was ennobled and child-rearing was forever changed.

> WORK ITSELF, OFTEN SEEN AS DRUDGERY, WAS REVEALED IN JESUS CHRIST AS HOLY, WHEN JOINED TO THE ONE WHO FASHIONED THE ENTIRE UNIVERSE.

That is because God came among us in Jesus Christ, and the entire human experience was transformed through His presence. First, He took up residence in a womb, making it a tabernacle of flesh. The work of redemption began *in utero*.

Throughout the entirety of His life, Jesus was redeeming and transforming the world. Heaven touched earth from the moment that the "Word became flesh and made his dwelling among us" (John 1:14). Through the incarnation of Jesus Christ, the entirety of the human experience was elevated and made new through Jesus Christ, fully God and fully man.

A WOMAN FULL OF GRACE

God Incarnate made His first home in the womb of a woman who said yes to the invitation of grace. She thus became a woman who was "full of grace." Jesus was reared by an earthly mother who spoke words of love to Him; she wiped His tears and caressed Him. She fed Him at her breast, washed His face, and groomed Him. She thus "mothered" the God of the whole human race who, in Jesus Christ, came into our midst as one of us. This is heart of the Christian faith.

Jesus worked with His hands, learned a trade, and sweated from the strain of hard work. Ah, the beauty and mystery of it all! The human experience was "super-naturalized" in the humanity of Jesus Christ; the ordinary was made extraordinary. Work itself, often seen as drudgery, was revealed in Jesus Christ as holy, when joined to the One who fashioned the entire universe. The entirety of our human experience became the path to our holiness and transformation, when it is lived in the One who lived it for us all. Everything He did, every word He spoke, He did and spoke as true God and true man, in the words of the ancient creed. While Jesus' disciples spent three years with Him during His "public ministry," Mary spent thirty-three years.

Mary was the first evangelist, bearing witness of Christ's incarnation to her cousin Elizabeth. She won the first convert *in utero,* in the person of John the Baptist. This event, traditionally called The Visitation, is recorded in the gospel of Saint Luke (Luke 1:39–45). It was crowned by her humble, obedient response to the angel's message—her *Fiat.* That response was not a one-time reaction. It was an expression of surrender that spanned all the years of her life, and we will consider it carefully in Part One of this book.

MARY'S SONG OF PRAISE

Mary's words to Elizabeth, upon which we will reflect in Part Two, are found in a hymn-like passage (Luke 1:46–55), often called the *Magnificat*. We will see how the world was turned upside down, not only by Mary's song of praise, but by her Son, whose redemptive mission that song foreshadows.

In the years that followed the Annunciation (when the angel Gabriel appeared to Mary and told her she was to bear the Son of God) and Nativity (His birth), as we'll see in Part Three, Mary was with Jesus on several significant occasions. One was the wedding at Cana, when the first of His miracles occurred in a special way in response to her intercession and out of the love of God, perfectly present in Jesus Christ. Then, as now, she offered the sage and still relevant advice, "Do whatever he tells you" (John 2:5).

At the end of her recorded history, Mary was present on the great day of pentecost, the birthday of the Church. Along with Jesus' other disciples, she encountered the outpouring of the Holy Spirit that empowered the early believers' missionary vocation. Mary understood something about the Spirit of God; she had been overshadowed by His wonderful presence when she was first visited by the angel. Both of those events equipped her to live her whole life in complete surrender to God's will and prefigured the mission of the entire Christian community.

As we will see, the Song of Mary—expressed in her *Fiat, Magnificat*, and the insights Scripture offers about her way of life—is about living a life of surrendered love. It is about encountering God relationally, personally, and intimately. It is about receiving, giving, receiving, giving; an exchange that means becoming a person for others, by entering more fully into the way of Jesus Christ and offering ourselves, in Him, for others. Mary teaches us about offering the *Fiat*—our humble yes—whenever the Lord speaks.

WALKING IN MARY'S WAY

As Pastor Hayford said, today's Christians, indeed all people of goodwill, need Mary's example in our present age, which is characterized by pride, arrogance, power, and self-aggrandizement. Her pattern of prayer and song reveals the fabric of her entire life. When we learn to walk in Mary's Way, which really is the way of her Son and Savior, we find the meaning of life itself. We, too, are called to respond to the gift of Love initiated by a loving God. Living in love is what Christian Scripture calls the "more excellent way" (1 Cor. 12:31). Mary understood and walked this way with remarkable humility.

Is it any wonder that the early Christians painted her image in the catacombs during their moments of fear, persecution, and doubt? Then, as now, they found great inspiration from this woman of great faith. When we reflect on Mary's yes to God, we come to understand that ordinary people can change human history. Like Christians in every era, Mary inspires us to add our own yes, our own *Fiat,* to hers.

The writings of the early church fathers are replete with reflections on Mary, who said very little in the biblical text. Indeed, none of our spiritual lives consists in an abundance of our words but rather in our receptivity to the Word-made-flesh. As we will discover, the earliest Christians called Mary the Second Eve, the mother of a new creation, because in her womb was carried the One whom the biblical authors would call the new Adam. Jesus Christ was born from her as the first-born of a new race of men and women, those who would themselves come to find a second birth through His life, death, and resurrection.

An early Christian council gave to Mary the name that will forever set her apart from all others in the eyes of believers: *Theotokos*, which means God-bearer or Mother of God. She alone carried within her womb the second person of the holy Trinity. She also carried Him in her heart. So can we. We can all become fountains of His Spirit for others. He resides within, and lives through, all of those who respond to the invitation of love as Mary did.

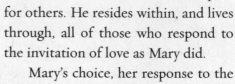

MARY ALONE CAR-
RIED WITHIN HER
WOMB THE SECOND
PERSON OF THE HOLY
TRINITY. SHE ALSO
CARRIED HIM IN HER
HEART. SO CAN WE.

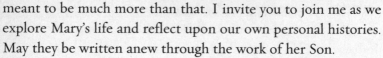

Mary's choice, her response to the invitation of a God who always respects human freedom, is a singular event in all of human history. However, it is meant to be much more than that. I invite you to join me as we explore Mary's life and reflect upon our own personal histories. May they be written anew through the work of her Son.

Mary is a monument of love
    which teaches all virtues.
She is our model.

We will never be able to understand
    Mary's greatness!
She is totally clothed by God's Word.

It is written of Her that
    she "stored up all these
    things in her heart" (Luke 2:51),
    and this means that She was living all those things . . .

When we try to love and this love becomes reciprocal,
    Christ lives among two or more persons.
Then we can offer Jesus spiritually to the world
    as Mary has given Jesus physically.

—CHIARA LUBICH

What came about in bodily form in Mary, the fullness of the godhead shining through Christ in the Blessed Virgin, takes place in a similar way in every soul that has been made pure. The Lord does not come in bodily form, for "we no longer know Christ according to the flesh," but He dwells in us spiritually and the Father takes up His abode with him, the Gospel tells us. In this way the child Jesus is born in each one of us.

—GREGORY OF NYSSA (A.D. 330–395, "ON VIRGINITY,"
PAGES 46, 324, AND 836)

PART ONE

The *Fiat*

MARY SAID, "BEHOLD, I AM THE HANDMAID OF THE LORD. MAY IT BE DONE TO ME ACCORDING TO YOUR WORD." THEN THE ANGEL DEPARTED FROM HER. (LUKE 1:38)

CHAPTER ONE

A WAY
OF HOLINESS

I am the handmaid of the Lord. May it be done to me according to your word. (Luke 1:38)

I am the handmaid of the Lord. May it be done to me according to your word" (Luke 1:38). Human history was forever changed when Mary spoke those words. They came from a deep spiritual reservoir within the heart of a young Jewish girl who was in love with the God of her fathers—Abraham, Isaac, and Jacob. Mary's yes to her Lord is called the *Fiat,* which in Latin means "let it be done."

Mary's *Fiat* was spoken from a heart filled with pure love for God. In a biblical context, *heart* is a word that means much more than the fleshy organ at the center of our chest cavity. It refers to our center, our core, the place where our deepest identity is rooted and from which our fundamental choices in life are made.

Mary's words proceeded from her heart, and it was a humble heart. This young woman was not full of herself, not self-protective, not cynical. She was, therefore, able to completely surrender herself *in* love, *to* love. Her initial assent to the angel Gabriel's announcement reveals the very meaning of another biblical word: *holy.* Holiness is not about being religious or looking pious. It is about being selfless. Mary was holy. Her life shows us how to become holy too.

In the original languages, the words in holy Scripture that were translated into the English word *holy* mean "set apart" or "consecrated." They refer to people or things that are totally given over to God and His worship. If we want to be holy, we need to explore the meaning of these words and make them our own. In everyday language, these people or items involved in temple worship were entirely dedicated to God's service. It is in that sense that we, too, are called to be set apart for the living God. We are to make a place for Him within ourselves and within the world. We are to bear His message through a lifestyle that radiates His love.

It is only by embracing ideas of being set apart and consecrated that our own personal histories can be truly transformed. This happens through conversion, or *metanoia,* which means "to change." Our hope for change, for becoming holy, is to open our lives to the One who is the source of all goodness and holiness. We are called to respond to His invitation, to say yes to a relationship with Him. This is what Mary's *Fiat* is all about. In saying yes to God, as Mary did, we are able to discover the path to conversion, to holiness, to authentic spirituality.

> IN SAYING YES TO GOD, AS MARY DID, WE ARE ABLE TO DISCOVER THE PATH TO CONVERSION, TO HOLINESS, TO AUTHENTIC SPIRITUALITY.

Our call to embrace the *Fiat* and to make it ours is not a formula for easy spiritual growth, nor is it the first in a series of steps that lead to solving the problems of life. The *Fiat* is not the answer to a riddle or the meaning behind some mystery. Bookstores are filled with how-to books. This is not one of them.

The spiritual life is a path, a way, and it involves a continuing, ongoing walk with the Lord. He has invited each of us into an intimate, personal exchange of love. This kind of intimacy with a living, loving God is the interior meaning of Mary's *Fiat,* her *Magnificat,* and her way of life. When we embrace Mary's Song and make it our own, we allow the One whom Mary bore in her body to be incarnated in and through us too.

Each of us can say yes to God. Each of us can respond with our entire being, with a *Fiat* of surrendered love. When we do so, our positive response marks the beginning of our participation in the very life of the God who is Father, Son, and Holy Spirit. We become sons and daughters of the Most High and enter into the life of the living God. In Him, we find our deepest identity, our real selves, through our participation in the One who made us, who redeems us, and who transforms us by His continual grace. Our holiness comes through touching the holy God, through being filled with His life and love.

Conversion begins when we say *Fiat* with our words and our deeds. It introduces us to a new and dynamic way of living *with* God and *in* God. As we lose ourselves in Him, we find ourselves again. We are made new and complete. This holy exchange—our life for His—is the essence of the spiritual journey. It is not about power but powerlessness. It is not about increase but decrease. It is not about becoming greater but becoming smaller.

In short, true spirituality is about surrender.

Centuries of Christian people have learned that as we lose ourselves in God, something significant happens. He reveals Himself as a God who can, does, and will act in the reality of our daily, human experiences. He makes it possible for us to have a genuine relationship, a dialogue, with Him. He certainly wants us to live life to the fullest. It is precisely because we were made for Him that we find our fulfillment in emptying ourselves, in selflessness. Then, of course, we are both filled and fulfilled in Him. (This is a fruit and not a goal, however. *He* is the goal.)

Mary's prayer teaches us to stay afloat in the ocean of life, with all of its undertows. Mary's Way is to become an ark within. When we do this, the same God who became incarnate within her takes up His residence in us. He comes to dwell in all men and women who say yes to Him.

Mary's prayer is an invitation to participate in the ongoing incarnation of God's love, for the sake of world. It is an invitation to live a life of redemption. In living a surrendered life, we not only are transformed ourselves, but we also participate in the mediation of God's love to others. The ongoing creative and redemptive work of God's love continues through us as we learn how to become arks, or dwelling places, through which love comes alive for all those around us.

We enter into Christ's incarnation as we participate in the prayer of Mary. But first, we must hear God's invitation. We must learn to listen for it with our whole hearts. Then, we can respond the same way Mary did: "Behold, I am the handmaid of the Lord. May it be done to me according to your word" (Luke 1:38).

> MARY'S PRAYER TEACHES US TO STAY AFLOAT IN THE OCEAN OF LIFE, WITH ALL OF ITS UNDERTOWS. MARY'S WAY IS TO BECOME AN ARK WITHIN.

God takes the initiative. He may whisper to our hearts through His Holy Spirit, or He may speak through His chosen messenger, but it is God who initiates and then awaits our response. Mary, in her selflessness, was open to the angel's visit. She recognized who was speaking. She listened, received, and responded. In so doing, she demonstrated the framework of all authentic spirituality. God initiates a relationship, and we respond in surrender to Him. This dynamic, this heavenly road, leads to a dialogue, a conversation, a way of life. By saying yes, through our own *Fiat,* we are set apart. Consecrated. Made holy.

Mary shows us *that* way.

Chapter Two

A Way
of Beauty

How beautiful upon the mountains are the feet of him who brings glad tidings. (Isa. 52:7)

C an you picture the scene when the angel Gabriel appeared to Mary? Most historians place Mary's age between thirteen and fifteen at the time. Just imagine what it must have been like for her.

I have had the honor and challenge of raising three daughters (along with two sons) through that most awkward and challenging season of their lives, their teenage years. I love them all deeply. I have to admit, I am not sure how any of my daughters would respond if visited or confronted by the angel Gabriel. For that matter, I am not sure how I would respond.

In the Christian tradition, the encounter between Mary and the angel is referred to as the Annunciation. It has become the backdrop for some of the most breathtaking artwork in human history, depicting the messenger sent by God to announce what He was about to do, not only in Mary, but in the world. It is a beautiful story, and it evokes beautiful images in our minds.

Because she was open to the invitation of God, Mary was prepared for her encounter with the angel. She expected to hear from God. She was a woman of prayer, and prayer had prepared her to respond to God with a surrendered spirit. Prayer had paved the way for her life of humility and service.

Mary's attitude cannot be contrived. It comes as a fruit of a genuine relationship with the God who sends His messengers to those who stay close to Him, who live their lives in an ongoing conversation with Him. This kind of experience can only take place through the exercise of faith.

This way of faith begins with the acceptance that there is a personal God who cares not only about the whole world, but about *your* world and *my* world. He is a merciful God who communicates His love through visitations in our own lives. In fact, it is a part of the most ancient of Christian traditions that each of us has a specific angel, a guardian, assigned to protect and direct us throughout our days. I believe that this is much more than piety—it is reality.

In cultivating our inner listening skills, our spiritual ears, we also find that our eyes are opened to see life differently. We get new eyes, the eyes of faith, like Mary had. We begin to see God's grace in all that surrounds us.

I have been around people who are, like Mary, really "full of grace." Perhaps you have too. They are truly beautiful people. That does not mean that they are physically attractive, at least in our contemporary Western understanding, though sometimes they are. Rather, they radiate a deeper spiritual beauty that flows from their participation with God, the source of all beauty. Perhaps one of the most beautiful women of our age was a little bent nun from Calcutta. Her name was Teresa, and most of us can conjure in our minds her markedly wrinkled face. The world still marvels at her life. She was clearly full of grace, and she was truly beautiful.

> IN CULTIVATING OUR INNER LISTENING SKILLS, OUR SPIRITUAL EARS, WE ALSO FIND THAT OUR EYES ARE OPENED TO SEE LIFE DIFFERENTLY.

Nothing was said in the biblical record about Mary's physical appearance, but her response to the angel tells us a lot about her. If we are full of grace, that grace changes us from the inside out, making us look more like the One who has come to dwell within us. God, after all, is the source of true beauty. Mary, who was full of grace, was very beautiful.

Mary had beautiful eyes.

I know this from the striking iconography of the Eastern Church and from the treasures of the sacred art of the West, both of which I have cherished all of my life. But I know it on a deeper level because of what I know about Mary. Through her beautiful eyes, she was able to see the angel, and thereby to behold the One he represented.

Mary had beautiful ears.

Mary's ears were open and attentive. They were able to hear the message sent by the angel—a message so profound that it would forever change her, the world around her, and all of human history (back to the beginning and forward until the end). The message Mary heard was an invitation of love addressed to the entire human race. When the message came to her, Mary was listening.

Mary had a beautiful heart.

I know this because she freely referred to herself as a handmaid of the Lord. She spoke words of voluntary servitude, expressing her surrender, love, and humility. Mary of Nazareth had not a trace of arrogance or haughtiness within her. It was precisely because she was emptied of self that she was full of grace.

Mary had beautiful feet.

The ancient Hebrew prophet Isaiah proclaimed:

> How beautiful upon the mountains
>   are the feet of him who brings glad tidings,
> Announcing peace, bearing good news,
>   announcing salvation, and saying to Zion,
> "Your God is King!" (Isa. 52:7)

This young Hebrew woman, immediately after pronouncing her *Fiat*, hurried to visit her kinswoman Elizabeth, the wife of Zechariah (Luke 1:39–40). Their visit was, in fact, the connection between the *Fiat* and the *Magnificat*.

Elizabeth herself was miraculously pregnant, late in life, carrying in her womb the forerunner of Christ, Saint John the Baptist. When Elizabeth heard Mary's greeting, the baby leaped inside her, and Elizabeth was filled with the Holy Spirit. In a loud voice she exclaimed, "Most blessed are you among women, and blessed is the fruit of your womb. And how does this happen to me, that the mother of my Lord should come to me? For at the moment the sound of your greeting reached my ears, the infant in my womb leaped for joy. Blessed are you who believed that what was spoken to you by the Lord would be fulfilled" (Luke 1:41–45).

It was during this meeting with Elizabeth that Mary broke into her song, the canticle called the *Magnificat*. She was the kind of messenger that the great Hebrew prophet Isaiah had spoken of. She truly was blessed among women, the first Christian evangelist. Her beautiful feet were, as Saint Paul wrote, fitted with "readiness for the gospel of peace" (Eph. 6:15).

Mary had beautiful arms and hands.

The Creator of the entire universe allowed His only begotten Son to be held, cared for, and nurtured by Mary. How blessed are the mother's arms that cradled God as a helpless child, carried Him in His youth, comforted Him during His adolescence, and continued to serve Him throughout those years at Nazareth where He "advanced (in) wisdom and age and favor before God and man" (Luke 2:52).

With her hands and arms, Mary embraced and caressed God, met His needs in His sacred humanity, dried His eyes, and combed His hair. With those arms and hands she tidied up the dwelling place of the glory that, in human form, had filled the temple.

Mary had a beautiful heart.

Mary's heart was broken. We see this in Michelangelo's masterpiece of the Mother of Sorrows, the Pietà. That eloquent marble image captures Mary's indescribable pain as she held Jesus' broken body and wept. A sword had indeed pierced her heart (Luke 2:35).

Mary had a beautiful face.

The wonderful God to whom she had surrendered her entire life allowed her to see Him face-to-face; to behold His face incarnate in His Son whom she bore and nurtured, cared for and worshipped. The Hebrew Scriptures tell us that when God spoke to Moses, He spoke "face to face, as one man speaks to another" (Ex. 33:11). This was an unprecedented event for the Hebrew people. Under the old covenant, no person could see God and live. When Moses came down from the mountain after encountering God, his face radiated the glory, and those around him were afraid to look (Ex. 34:29–30).

Mary beheld Him daily. When she kissed His face, her own face must have radiated the love that flowed from Jesus. Saint Paul would write to the Christians in Corinth that the glory of God was revealed in the face of Christ (2 Cor. 4:6).

> WHETHER MARY IS ENVISIONED AS A JEWISH MAIDEN, YOUNG MEXICAN, ASIAN, OR AFRICAN WOMAN, IT MATTERS LITTLE. HER BEAUTY TRANSCENDS AND TRANSFORMS EVERY CULTURAL DEFINITION OF BEAUTY, BECAUSE IT REFLECTS THE VERY BEAUTY OF GOD.

Mary beheld His face continuously, from the tiny face of an infant through every stage of His human life, until she saw that face of love bloodied and bruised as He cried out, "It is finished" (John 19:30).

Is it any wonder that Christians throughout the ages have always depicted Mary as a beautiful woman? Whether she is envisioned as a Jewish maiden, young Mexican, Asian, or African woman, it matters little. Her beauty transcends and transforms every cultural definition of beauty, because it reflects the very beauty of God.

As we consider Mary's beauty, we need to look at her through the eyes of faith. Recently, after ruefully acknowledging that I wasn't seeing as well as I used to, I purchased some reading glasses. I will never forget the experience of putting on those glasses. Suddenly, I could see every letter printed on the products in front of me, and countless other details I hadn't noticed before. The world literally looked different.

This is what happens to those of us who choose to view reality through faith's lens. A new vision dawns in our lives like the morning light, brightening our paths. It changes, clarifies, and expands our horizons, allowing us to see everything from a fresh perspective. As we learn to see Mary's life through the eyes of faith, it also becomes possible for us to entertain angels ourselves.

CHAPTER THREE

A WAY
OF GRACE

In the sixth month, the angel Gabriel was sent from God to a town of Galilee called Nazareth, to a virgin betrothed to a man named Joseph, of the house of David, and the virgin's name was Mary. And coming to her, he said, "Hail, favored one! The Lord is with you." (Luke 1:26–28)

S cripture tells us that Mary was favored. She walked in a deep, abiding relationship with God, and He was with her *before* she responded to His invitation. Because of her predisposition to His grace, God chose Mary even before Mary chose God. The order is vitally important if we are to truly begin to grasp the deeper meaning of the spiritual life.

We sometimes think that we have brought or allowed God into our lives. This is evident in the way some Christian groups describe our early walk with the Lord. By emphasizing that we need to first "invite" the Lord into our lives, the use of popular language can actually lead us to believe that we do the initiating and therefore control the relationship. In fact, nothing could be further from the truth.

Jesus made this clear in these words to His disciples: "It was not you who chose me, but I who chose you" (John 15:16). All too often, in our religious subcultures, we actually communicate the opposite. Whether it is through an emphasis on a specific prayer required as a preliminary step, or a limited concept of the nature of grace, we may unwittingly communicate the notion that our words or our actions actually bring God into our lives. We imply that He is reluctant to act, or dependent upon our invitation.

I was raised in a sacramental tradition as a Catholic. My family practiced their faith until a tragedy shook our foundations. Afterward we remained cultural but not practicing Catholics. This happened as I began my turbulent teenage years.

A few years later, when I returned to the practice of my

faith, I felt that I had come home. I thought that I had "found" the Lord. In a sense, that was true. However, I would come to discover that He had never left me. It was I who had wandered away, although it took a while to understand what that meant as His grace unfolded in my daily life.

During that time I discovered the prayer that Augustine, one of the great Western church fathers, uttered upon his own return to faith. He recorded this prayer in his *Confessions:*

> Late have I loved you, O Beauty ever ancient, ever new, late have I loved you! You were within me, but I was outside, and it was there that I searched for you.
> In my unloveliness I plunged into the lovely things which you created. You were with me, but I was not with you. Created things kept me from you; yet if they had not been in you they would have not been at all. You called, you shouted, and you broke through my deafness. You flashed, you shone, and you dispelled my blindness. You breathed your fragrance on me; I drew in breath and now I pant for you. I have tasted you, now I hunger and thirst for more. You touched me, and I burned for your peace.

Augustine of Hippo understood, like Mary and countless others through the ages, that it is the Lord who reaches out in love. It is the Lord who offers His grace. We are the recipients of that grace, and it fills us according to the capacity He has built within us. The proper order of initiation and response has profound relevance for us if we desire to live the spiritual life. Our God is already there. He awaits our response to His relentless love and grace, which are both within and all around us.

We can learn many more things from the angel's visit to Mary. Her experience with Gabriel offers important lessons for our own daily lives.

First of all, the story is time specific. The angel came in the sixth month of Elizabeth's pregnancy. Angels still come at the specific moment that God chooses to intervene in our lives. He is outside of time but always on time. He doesn't wear a watch, keep a day-timer, or use a pocket computer. Still, He is never early or late.

Next, angels appear to specific people in the real circumstances of their daily lives, in the midst of their human relationships. The angel came particularly to "a virgin betrothed to a man named Joseph." The more I grow in grace myself, the more I am able to recognize the angels, or messengers, the Lord sends into my life. They come bearing His message, speaking to my specific circumstances at a specific time of need.

> ANGELS STILL COME AT THE SPECIFIC MOMENT THAT GOD CHOOSES TO INTERVENE IN OUR LIVES. HE IS OUTSIDE OF TIME BUT ALWAYS ON TIME.

The angelic greeting tells us a lot about Mary, but also about our own invitation into a relationship with God. Gabriel's greeting was specific. Mary was addressed by her Hebrew name, implying that the God from whom the angel was sent knew Mary personally and had a relationship with her that preceded the visitation. So it is with each of us. As the great Hebrew psalmist David sang,

> *You formed my inmost being; you knit me in my mother's womb.*
>
> *I praise you, so wonderfully you made me; wonderful are your works! My very self you knew; my bones were not hidden from you, when I was being made in secret, fashioned as in the depths of the earth. Your eyes foresaw my actions; in your book all are written down; my days were shaped, before one came to be. (Ps. 139:13–16)*

As we have seen, the angel refers to Mary as "O highly favored one" or, in other translations, "full of grace." These words also form the introduction to a popular prayer in my own church tradition that I have treasured since my youth: "Hail Mary, full of grace, the Lord is with thee." Mary was indeed favored and full of grace. The Lord of heaven and earth had prepared and chosen her as a fertile ground into which He planted the seed of His Word. When we respond to the words of the Lord, we also become filled with grace as He is formed within us.

Angels still visit those who understand grace as the favor and blessing of God. They bring God's message to people humble enough to open themselves to its dynamic, sanctifying, and transforming action. Perhaps the reason the Scriptures tell us so little about Mary was because she was meant to serve as a mirror, a reflection, of someone much more important. It was His grace that filled her.

> PERHAPS THE REASON THE SCRIPTURES TELL US SO LITTLE ABOUT MARY WAS BECAUSE SHE WAS MEANT TO SERVE AS A MIRROR, A REFLECTION, OF SOMEONE MUCH MORE IMPORTANT.

God brings new life to ordinary people who have eyes to see, ears to hear, and pure hearts that are opened to His invitation of love. They, like Mary, become full of grace through their encounter with their Creator. Mary of Nazareth's witness made a profound mystery wonderfully simple. She lived a fruitful life, marked by an innocent and childlike spirit. As Jesus said, "I give you praise, Father, Lord of heaven and earth, for although you have hidden these things from the wise and the learned you have revealed them to the childlike" (Luke 10:21). His words help us understand that we, too, are to become as little children.

Each of us is called to become full of grace. The Lord desires to be with us, to live within us in a world that hungers for His love—love that can be borne in us and offered through us. Mary showed us the way. She heard the promise, believed, was filled with grace, and conceived the Lord who is love incarnate. We can do likewise if we learn to pray, listen, hear, respond, and say yes. In doing so we, like Mary, will discover that nothing is impossible with God.

Such light,
Such luminous colors!
The memory blurs my view
Of our dusty street,
Our poor drab village;
The joy of it all catches in my throat
In exquisite yearning
Aching like a long-forgotten song.
And that voice, unlike any other—
Even now it speaks in my soul,
"Nothing is impossible . . ."
Even now I hear it
As my breasts swell and ache
As my belly grows round
As my body trembles with new life.

Mother's eyes are dark with worry
Joseph's face is drawn with grief
Oh my God, how will I tell them?
Can I face their disbelief?

—*Lela Gilbert*

CHAPTER FOUR

A WAY
OF THE
IMPOSSIBLE

But Mary said to the angel, "How can this be, since I have no relations with a man?" And the angel said to her in reply, "The holy Spirit will come upon you, and the power of the Most High will overshadow you. Therefore the child to be born will be called holy, the Son of God. And behold, Elizabeth, your relative, has also conceived a son in her old age, and this is the sixth month for her who was called barren; for nothing will be impossible for God." (Luke 1:34–37)

When the living God visits people, He makes the impossible entirely possible. Still, He never violates our human freedom. He waits for us to respond. He waits for us to believe that nothing is impossible for Him. In so believing, we become the people He knows we can be. The God who is love yearns for our loving response, yet He has ordained that love be freely and voluntarily given. Love never coerces, but instead invites a response.

How impractical the spiritual life often seems to the contemporary mind. Bishop Alvaro del Portillo has written, "The so-called 'practical people' are not really the most useful in the service of Christ's Church, nor are those who merely expound theories. Rather it is the true contemplatives who best serve her; those with the steady generous and passionate desire of transfiguring and divinizing all creation with Christ and in Christ. It may sound paradoxical, but in the Church of Jesus Christ, the mystic is the only practical person."

Mary's *Fiat* invites us to listen for the voice of God. When we learn to listen, we begin to hear His wooing, His loving invitation into an authentic, ongoing, consuming, transforming, and intimate relationship with Him. The God who created us knows who we are. This God will redeem us in His Son. This God will transform us through His Spirit, but only if we listen to His voice and say yes to His invitation.

Mary provided a practical example for surrendering to a relationship with God. Such a concept is a paradox to the modern mind, insisting as it does on such seemingly asymmetrical notions. Surrendering to God's ways means losing our life in order to find it. It means giving up ourselves through love in order to discover who we are meant to become. Of all creation, only people can give themselves away in love as Jesus Christ did. We do so by exercising the part of ourselves that is made in God's image—our capacity for freedom. Love has to be a continuously free choice, a choice made daily, hourly, moment-by-moment.

> OF ALL CREATION, ONLY PEOPLE CAN GIVE THEMSELVES AWAY IN LOVE AS JESUS CHRIST DID.

The gospel of John tells us, "God so loved the world that he gave . . ." (John 3:16). What did He give? He gave His Son. He still gives His Son today through the family that His Son draws to Himself. In the Genesis story of Eden, God's first earthly family was driven away from Him by sin at the Tree of Knowledge of Good and Evil. God draws us back to Himself at the second tree, the tree of surrendered love, the cross of Calvary. There we witness the greatest act of surrendered love, the complete gift of love Himself, offered up to the entire human race.

The same God who spoke to Mary offers to every one of us the invitation into a relationship. He is able to accomplish in us and through us what we may conceive of as impossible, or as Saint Paul wrote in Ephesians 3:20, "more than all we ask or imagine." In fact, He promises that the impossible will be possible to those who believe. He never lies. He makes this promise not only on our behalf, but for the sake of the world. He still loves the world so much that He continues to send His Son, through you and me, on His mission as the Redeemer. He participates in the Lord's redemptive mission as His church.

Surrendered love is the very essence of faith and, indeed, of life itself. It may seem impractical in our mundane lives, to think about living by faith and not by sight. It may seem impractical to listen for God's inner voice. But He wants to transform our lives from mundane to miraculous.

The God who is love wants us to receive, to learn, and to live in His love. He continues to reveal its deeper implications in the lives of very real people who are truly spiritual. They make heaven touch earth the way Jesus did. When heaven touches earth, amazing things happen all around us. Still today, Mary's story demonstrates total openness to God's invitation of love, an openness that resulted in her becoming the first living tabernacle of love incarnate, Jesus Christ. Through the virgin birth of God's only begotten Son, Mary proved to us that with God, there's no such thing as impossible.

CHAPTER FIVE

A WAY
OF LOVE

Strive eagerly for the greatest spiritual gifts. But I shall show you a still more excellent way. If I speak in human and angelic tongues but do not have love, I am a resounding gong or a clashing cymbal. And if I have the gift of prophecy and comprehend all mysteries and all knowledge; if I have all faith so as to move mountains but do not have love, I am nothing. If I give away everything I own, and if I hand my body over so that I may boast but do not have love, I gain nothing. Love is patient, love is kind. It is not jealous, (love) is not pompous, it is not inflated, it is not rude, it does not seek its own interests, it is not quick-tempered, it does not brood over injury, it does not rejoice over wrongdoing but rejoices with the truth. It bears all things, believes all things, hopes all things, endures all things. Love never fails. If there are prophecies, they will be brought to nothing; if tongues, they will cease; if knowledge, it will be brought to nothing. For we know partially and we prophesy partially, but when the perfect comes, the partial will pass away. When I was a child, I used to talk as a child, think as a child, reason as a child; when I became a man, I put aside childish things. At present we see indistinctly, as in a mirror, but then face to face. At present I know partially; then I shall know fully, as I am fully known. So faith, hope, love remain, these three; but the greatest of these is love. (1 Cor. 12:31—13:13)

When Saint Paul's words were penned, the young Corinthian Christians were quite taken with themselves. They were feeling somewhat smug and reveling in the manifestations of spiritual gifts in their own midst. Comparing their attitude to contemporary times, there really *is* nothing new under the sun (Eccl. 1:9). Paul's words need to be revisited in our religious communities today. In fact, they need to be understood by all of us who would walk the way of love as Mary did. If we desire to be more than a "resounding gong or a clashing cymbal," we need to come to know Jesus, who is love personified. We need to become like Him, who by His very love created the whole universe and re-creates it through His cross and Resurrection.

Saint Paul reminded the Christians in Galatia that our loving God became incarnate, taking on human flesh and living among us: "But when the fullness of time had come, God sent his Son, born of a woman, born under the law, to ransom those under the law, so that we might receive adoption. As proof that you are children, God sent the spirit of his Son into our hearts, crying out, 'Abba, Father!' So you are no longer a slave but a child, and if a child then also an heir, through God" (Gal. 4:4–7).

The Son of God holds His own sons and daughters in an embrace of grace. Within that embrace, He communicates Himself to us every moment. The surest way to experience that kind of intimate relationship with Him is to learn to pray. But how? Interestingly, the first thing to do is stop talking. Silence is actually the beginning of real prayer. We've seen how essential listening is to spiritual formation. We see this clearly in Mary, who was a woman of few words, a woman of the Word, a woman who knew how to listen.

A contemporary mystic, Mother Teresa of Calcutta, said it this way:

> God is the friend of silence . . . in that silence he will listen to us; there he will speak to our soul, and there we will hear his voice. The fruit of silence is faith. The fruit of faith is prayer, the fruit of prayer is love, the fruit of love is service and the fruit of service is silence. In the silence of the heart God speaks. If you face God in prayer and silence, God will speak to you. Then you will know that you are nothing. It is only when you realize your nothingness, your empti-ness, that God can fill you with Himself. Silence gives us a new way of looking at everything. We need this silence in order to touch souls. God is the friend of silence. His language is silence: "Be still and know that I am God." (Ps. 46:10)

I am a Catholic clergyman. I love the high liturgical worship of my church in all of its grandeur, sign, and symbolism. In my life I have been touched by the grace of several renewal experiences. I am at home in many different kinds of personal and group prayer expressions. These expressions range from the enthusiasm of evangelical, pentecostal, and charismatic worship, to the deep and profound piety expressions of my own, and other, Christian traditions, including the beauty of orthodox Christianity.

I have, however, grown increasingly weary of the limited understanding and, in some instances, the arrogant chatter that accompanies some contemporary Christian expressions. We should take a second look at the presentations of prayer, worship, and Christian life that are modeled in our churches or presented over the media. What do they say to those who are seriously seeking to know God?

All too often, when I find myself channel surfing I stumble into some variations of the Christian faith depicted on television. I must admit experiencing a certain discouragement and sometimes a little anger. TV offers an odd Christian subculture, whose ambassadors speak in a language that few outside their small, closed circle can even understand. Sometimes I discern a sense of superiority behind the claims to power. Sometimes I wonder if they are afraid to stop talking. I have to ask, is that how Jesus spoke and acted?

Can you imagine what it was like to accompany God's Son when His sacred feet walked on the roads of Galilee? Biblical accounts tell us that people longed to be with Him; they flocked to Him, yearning just to touch the hem of His garment. The accounts are filled with people climbing trees, leaving nets and significant relationships, running as fast as they could to be with Him, hoping to catch a glimpse of Him. Jesus' sacred humanity attracted ordinary people of the earth like a warm blanket on a cold night.

> WE SHOULD TAKE A SECOND LOOK AT THE PRESENTATIONS OF PRAYER, WORSHIP, AND CHRISTIAN LIFE THAT ARE MODELED IN OUR CHURCHES OR PRESENTED OVER THE MEDIA. WHAT DO THEY SAY TO THOSE WHO ARE SERIOUSLY SEEKING TO KNOW GOD?

Today there are countless people truly seeking the great treasure of a relationship with God. They will not find Him in the noisy subcultures that claim to be the full representation of Christianity. They will not find Him in all the shouting and demanding. Love's voice is not found in bravado, but in brokenness. Human posturing is simply a mask, meant to hide our deepest fears. But rather than hiding those fears, we are invited to nail them, one by one, to Calvary's tree. At the cross we can receive, in exchange for our fears, the love of God.

Only at Golgotha can women and men can find the real beauty of God—a God who understands and empties Himself for us in crucified love. It is this God, stretching wounded hands out to embrace a world that has rejected Him, who wants a relationship of love with humankind. It is this God that Mary loved.

A Christian monk of the ninth century, Saint Theodore the Studite, once wrote:

> How precious the gift of the cross, how splendid to contemplate! In the cross there is no mingling of good and evil, as in the tree of paradise: it is wholly beautiful to behold and good to taste. The fruit of this tree is not death but life, not darkness but light. This tree does not cast us out of paradise but opens the way for our return.
>
> This was the tree on which Christ, like a king on a chariot, destroyed the devil, the lord of death, and freed the human race from his tyranny. This was the tree upon which the Lord, like a brave warrior wounded in hands, feet, and side, healed the wounds of sin that the evil serpent had inflicted on our nature. A tree once caused our death, but now a tree brings life. Once deceived by a tree, we have now repelled the cunning serpent by a tree. What an astonishing transformation! That death should become life, that decay should become immortality, and that shame should become glory!

Standing in silence at the foot of the cross, Mary stood watching. She did not shout, or cry out, or draw attention to herself.

Perhaps this is because she was not afraid. The beloved disciple John stood there with her. He later wrote in his first letter, "There is no fear in love, but perfect love drives out fear because fear has to do with punishment, and so one who fears is not yet perfect in love. We love because He first loved us" (1 John 4:18–19).

Mary had experienced the overshadowing and overwhelming love of God some thirty-three years before. Her heart was broken, pierced with a sword, yet she said yes once again at that cross. Through her lifelong *Fiat*, and by her presence at the foot of that tree, she demonstrated to us how to overcome the greatest obstacle to our own spiritual lives—fear. Mary was called to courage at the beginning of her journey, when the angel Gabriel spoke the words "do not be afraid" to her. Even now, she shows us how to overcome fear through her Son's perfect love. That love overcomes a multitude of sins.

The fear of failure impedes our willingness to risk for others.

The fear of being disappointed keeps us from reaching out to others.

The fear of death lies at the root of our inability to deal with others' suffering.

> THE FEAR OF DEATH LIES AT THE ROOT OF OUR INABILITY TO DEAL WITH OTHERS' SUFFERING.

Jesus addressed all our fears when He spoke to Jairus, a synagogue official whose daughter was dying. "Do not be afraid," Jesus said. "Just have faith" (Mark 5:36). We need to listen to those same words today. We need to hear them. We need to believe and to live them.

Even Mary, who found the courage to stand by the cross, was acquainted with fear. She had long ago learned to overcome it by faith. The biblical account says of her, "But she was greatly troubled at what was said and pondered what sort of greeting this might be. Then the angel said to her, 'Do not be afraid, Mary, for you have found favor with God'" (Luke 1:29–30).

Contemplation upon the life of Mary helps reveal the sources of our fears. Her humility and obedience, even in the face of disturbing prophecies and terrible threats, help us unmask fear's disguises, hidden deep within ourselves. Suffering, failure, struggle, and loss are not absent from the Christian's life. But, like Mary, we can move beyond fear and choose love. In so doing, we can learn to love more deeply and more genuinely than we have ever loved before.

CHAPTER SIX

A WAY
OF GIVING

History is not simply a fixed progression toward what is better—but rather, an event of freedom. Specifically, it is a struggle between freedoms that are in mutual conflict: a conflict between two loves—the love of God to the point of disregarding self and the love of self to the point of disregarding God. (John Paul II, Christian Family in the Modern World, *n. 6)*

The biblical texts say very little about Mary, and I believe that she would have wanted it that way. Instead, everything we know about her life pointed to her beloved Son and Savior. She didn't say much, but she said one word that changed all of human history. She said yes. The word proceeded from the pure heart of a simple woman who could have just as easily said no. Instead she gave herself. She completely surrendered herself to the God who had first given Himself to her.

The path of choosing God means participating in His self-emptying love. When we assent to His invitation, our own personal histories are forever changed, and we are made new. When we give ourselves to God, freely offering back to Him what He has offered to us, we discover the deepest possible meaning in our lives, our purpose as found in Him. We begin to truly live because we begin to truly love.

Emptying ourselves in obedience to God allows Christ to become "incarnate," to come into us and to live through each of us. Like Mary, we make a place for God. God respects His image in us, the *Imago Deo,* which is rooted and evident in our capacity to freely choose Him. Choosing to give ourselves away in love to God is the very essence, purpose, and meaning of human existence. Saying yes to God is the path to true peace, which, in the biblical sense, is about right relationships. Giving ourselves away to God opens the door to right relationships with Him, with one another, and with the entire universe that He has created.

Giving ourselves away to God is not a one-time event. Rather, it is a way of living and a way of loving. It is a call to communion.

This is the paradox: in losing our life we actually find it in Him, and He is its source. In fact, no one understands better than God who we are and what we are like. The New Testament author of the letter to the Hebrews wrote: "For we do not have a high priest who is unable to sympathize with our weaknesses, but one who has similarly been tested in every way, yet without sin" (Heb. 4:15).

The Eternal Word, coexistent with the Father and the Spirit, in the perfect unity that is trinitarian love, became a real man in real time and in real history. Against all odds, He began His earthly life within the womb of a teenage Jewish virgin. Even before His birth in Bethlehem, Jesus sanctified all mothers by dwelling within the first temple, the new ark of the new covenant, the womb of His beloved, self-chosen mother. This fact is not incidental. God did not choose Mary as a receptacle. He chose her as a mother. Is it any wonder that His choice has given rise to two millennia of theological, poetic, and artistic reflections? But it is, in fact, about much more. The Father has made it possible for us to allow His Son to be born in us as well, so that we, too, can give Him to the world.

> GIVING OURSELVES AWAY TO GOD IS NOT A ONE-TIME EVENT. RATHER, IT IS A WAY OF LIVING AND A WAY OF LOVING.

Our choice will not only affect the world around us, but will literally change us either for good or for ill. Gregory of Nyssa, an early Christian father, wrote: "Now, human life is always subject to change: it needs to be born ever anew . . . but here birth does not come about by a foreign intervention, as is the case with bodily beings, it is the result of a free choice. Thus we are in a certain way our own parents, creating ourselves as we will, by our decisions" (St. Gregory of Nyssa, *De vita Moysis,* II, 2–3; cited in *Veritatis splendor,* no. 71).

When we choose to give ourselves to God, to bear Christ within us, we are choosing to participate in a life of prayer, worship, and surrendered love. A friend of mine, Fr. Michael Scanlan, whose persistent prayer and heroic life helped to renew an entire college, always told me: "You live the way you pray, and you pray the way you live." He was correct.

We can learn about giving ourselves away by reflecting on Mary. The Christian life is not really about our increase at all. In fact, it is not about *us* at all. Mary's yes teaches us to decrease, to be little, to be hidden, so that the God of love may truly be manifest in and through us for the sake of others. Her example demonstrates a way to empty ourselves of ourselves so that we may be filled with the very life and presence of God for others.

We live in an age that has become intoxicated with the power of choice. However, there are deeper questions to be faced than whether we *can* choose. More important are what choices we make, and in the making, what kind of people are we choosing to become? Are we learning to give ourselves up so that we can receive all that God has for us? Mary gave up a predictable and acceptable place in her small town society to bear the Son of God for the world. It cost her dearly, but she gained heaven in the process.

> THERE ARE DEEPER QUESTIONS TO BE FACED THAN WHETHER WE CAN CHOOSE. MORE IMPORTANT ARE WHAT CHOICES WE MAKE, AND IN THE MAKING, WHAT KIND OF PEOPLE ARE WE CHOOSING TO BECOME?

Mary's *Fiat* was not a singular event. It issued forth into a life canticle, a song, a prayer, a way, and a life that we are invited to emulate and make our own. After Mary's yes, the biblical account reveals her breaking forth into song. That song is the *Magnificat*, which is a Latin word that means to "magnify" or "extol." Mary's hymn of praise responds to the great gift of love that became hers as a result of her *Fiat.* She became the bearer of Christ, because the very life of God came to dwell within her. She chose Him every day, every minute, and in so doing she revealed Him to others. So must we.

In the pages that follow, we will listen to the song that Mary sang in her cousin Elizabeth's house. We will try to understand the interior meaning of its verses, the pure beauty of its melody. With God's help, we will learn to sing Mary's Song, and her way of giving can become our way too.

He woke me,
Unborn and silent,
Still he woke me to a symphony of crickets,
To a star-strewn sky
To the warm nightwind:
His crickets, his stars, his wind,
And the hand that made them
Stirred within me like a greeting from a friend.
What does he feel? What does he know?
Does he know me?
Does he already know my name?

—*Lela Gilbert*

PART TWO

The *Magnificat*

My soul proclaims the greatness of the Lord;
  my spirit rejoices in God my savior.
For he has looked upon his handmaid's lowliness;
  behold, from now on will all ages call me blessed.
The Mighty One has done great things for me,
  and holy is his name.
His mercy is from age to age
  to those who fear him.
He has shown might with his arm,
  dispersed the arrogant of mind and heart.
He has thrown down the rulers from their
thrones
  but lifted up the lowly.
The hungry he has filled with good things;
  the rich he has sent away empty.
He has helped Israel his servant,
  remembering his mercy,
according to his promise to our fathers,
  to Abraham and to his descendants forever.

(Luke 1:46–55)

CHAPTER SEVEN

KEEPING AN UNDIVIDED HEART

*My soul proclaims the greatness of the Lord; my spirit
rejoices in God my savior. (Luke 1:46–47)*

*Teach me, Lord, your way
    that I may walk in your truth,
    single-hearted and revering your name.
I will praise you with all my heart,
    glorify your name forever, Lord my God.
Your love for me is great. (Ps. 86:11–13)*

M ary's Song, *The Magnificat,* is profoundly personal. "My soul magnifies," she proclaims along with "my spirit rejoices." It is hard for many of us, particularly Westerners, to comprehend the meaning of this acclamation. Mary is teaching us about having a deep, all-encompassing, and completely integrated relationship with God. Young as she was, simple as her background may have been, Mary had a sense of self. She knew who she was, and because she owned herself, she could freely choose to give herself away to God in a life of surrendered love. Mary had an undivided heart.

In classical Christian teaching, only human beings are able to know and love their Creator. And only men and women are called to share, by knowledge and love, in God's own life. It was for this end that we were created, and this is the fundamental reason for our human dignity. Mary's own dignity was revealed in her freely made choice to love God with her whole body, soul, and spirit—her whole being.

The great Shema of Israel was recorded in the book of Deuteronomy: "Hear, O Israel! The LORD is our God, the LORD alone! Therefore, you shall love the LORD, your God, with all your heart, and with all your soul, and with all your strength" (Deut. 6:4–5). It is a call to give everything to God without reserve. As a daughter of the old covenant, Mary understood the Shema and was devoted to loving the Lord with her entire being. She showed us the way to do the same.

Mary exercised her God-given human freedom by choosing

to respond to the invitation of the Creator who had fashioned her for Himself. She demonstrated the freedom of choice we have in obeying the God who loves us and calls us to be His own. There is a reflexive nature to our capacity to choose God. It bears repeating: in our choosing we not only affect the world around us, but we also change ourselves.

We live in an age that clamors for the right to choose. Mistaken notions of choice as a raw power over others, or the so-called right to do anything we want, are all too common in a modern society that has lost its connection to God. This is not a new thing in the world. The Eden story is all about the errant exercise of freedom, the making of a wrong choice at the Tree of the Knowledge of Good and Evil in the garden. At the beginning of human history, God invited us into a communion of love. Sadly, we chose instead a counterfeit notion of freedom as the right to do whatever we want. In so doing, sin came into the world.

> IT BEARS REPEATING: IN OUR CHOOSING WE NOT ONLY AFFECT THE WORLD AROUND US, BUT WE ALSO CHANGE OURSELVES.

Christians proclaim that God's love became a person and made the ultimate choice on the second tree—Calvary's cross. There Jesus Christ died so that we might live. By voluntarily giving up His life, He freed us from the power of sin and death. The early fathers of the Church referred to Mary as the Second Eve, because her love and obedience opened the door for the new creation, accomplished through the life, death, and resurrection of her Son and Savior, Jesus Christ.

In A.D. 190, Irenaeus wrote: "Mary the Virgin is found to be obedient, saying: 'Behold, O Lord, your handmaid; be it done to me according to your word.' Eve, however, was disobedient; and when yet a virgin, she did not obey . . . having become disobedient, was made the cause of death for herself and for the whole human race; so also Mary, betrothed to a man but nevertheless still a virgin, being obedient, was made the cause of salvation for herself and for the whole human race . . . Thus, the knot of Eve's disobedience was loosed by the obedience of Mary. What the virgin Eve had bound in unbelief, the Virgin Mary loosed through faith" (St. Irenaeus, *Against Heresies*).

Mary's choice was for God, and she chose Him with her whole being. That is what "my soul magnifies" and "my spirit rejoices" is all about. That is how we are all to choose God. Following the Lord involves a radical re-orienting of our entire life. Faith is not a coat that we put on as we go into a church building and take off when we enter the public square. Choosing God requires that we make the choice just as Mary did, with her whole person.

Still, in our post-Cartesian, Western worldview, influenced as it has been by the division between the spiritual and the physical aspects of human life, we may not fully understand the anthropology of Mary. In fact, she lived a life rooted in an intuitive view of the human person. This should come as no surprise. She was, after all, a Jewish woman and a daughter of Abraham.

> FAITH IS NOT A COAT THAT WE PUT ON AS WE GO INTO A CHURCH BUILDING AND TAKE OFF WHEN WE ENTER THE PUBLIC SQUARE. CHOOSING GOD REQUIRES THAT WE MAKE THE CHOICE JUST AS MARY DID, WITH HER WHOLE PERSON.

When Mary spoke of her soul and her spirit, she was speaking of her essence, the core of her being. It was what philosophers call her "ontology." The Hebrew word, which is often translated "soul," is *nepes*, and it reveals the Jewish understanding of the human person. This *nepes*, this soul, infused Mary's entire being. It flowed through her blood and could not be separated from her body. It was with this soul that Mary magnified the Lord.

When we love the Lord our God with our entire mind, we commit to Him our thoughts, our beliefs, and our consciousness, the places in which we make willful decisions. We recognize that our capacity to think, to question, to reason, and to analyze is not a threat to faith but the very path to serious, sustaining, and life-changing faith.

When we love the Lord our God with all our strength, we bring our bodies into the plan for which we were fashioned. The Christian faith proclaims that we are going to have resurrected bodies in the life to come. Many in our generation seem to have lost respect for human dignity, for a holy and healthy view of human sexuality, and for the respect and dignity proper to the human body. Our bodies express not only who we are and who God is, but they are the vehicles through which we speak the language of love. This is one of the reasons Christians choose to fast, to lift their hands in worship, to cross themselves, to fall on their knees, or to prostrate themselves in prayer. They are bringing their bodies into full participation in worshipping the Creator.

When we love the Lord our God with all our heart, we offer our emotions and learn to love fully as human persons redeemed in Christ. Our emotions are meant to reflect who we are becoming as the work of His redemption continues within us, rather than serve as a wayward compass, directing us away from Him and His best plans for our lives.

This full integration of Mary's nature is both human and holy. It does not fall prey to the two approaches that are so often evident in contemporary spiritualities—either underemphasizing or overemphasizing physical, intellectual, or emotional concerns. The undivided heart integrates these extremes by engaging our whole being as a gift from God that should be given back to Him. In an integrated life, mind, body, soul, and spirit are connected to the root of our freedom, our faculty of choice. Each dimension of human life is a gift and a servant, not a master to dominate us, or a distraction to be avoided.

As a result of her undivided heart, Mary "magnified" God, a concept that captures Mary's Way. We have all used magnifying glasses. They increase the experience, the size, and the perception of what they magnify. So it was with Mary. She chose to decrease herself, so that in doing so, others could see instead the Lord whom she loved. The image of God, stamped upon her soul, was written boldly.

God has, in Jesus, touched all of us, beginning a process of transformation and restoration. God has called us to be integrated men and women who, like Mary, choose to love Him and magnify Him on the earth. This action of God in our lives, transforming us in love, is what redemption is all about. It is as whole people—body, soul, spirit—

> MARY CHOSE TO DECREASE HERSELF, SO THAT IN DOING SO, OTHERS COULD SEE INSTEAD THE LORD WHOM SHE LOVED. THE IMAGE OF GOD, STAMPED UPON HER SOUL, WAS WRITTEN BOLDLY.

that we are being saved. And it is in resurrected bodies, not as disembodied ghosts, that we will fully participate in the new heaven and new earth (Rev. 21). We will spend eternity in full communion with the God who is Father, Son, and Spirit—the holy Trinity of persons, dwelling in the perfect unity of love.

Chapter Eight

Making an Honest Self-Assessment

For he has looked upon his handmaid's lowliness. (Luke 1:48)

Without an undivided heart, we cannot freely choose God's way. Without humility, we cannot live an authentic spiritual life. Mary demonstrated the virtue of humility, which is the foundation of true human freedom. Humility keeps us from being enslaved by our egos and their constant demands. It serves as an antidote to the arrogance and the resulting despair of our present age. An honest self-assessment can guide us into an authentic relationship with the living God, who alone can fill the emptiness within our souls. As Saint Augustine prayed in his famous prayer, "You have made us for yourself, O Lord, and our hearts are restless until they rest in you" (*Confessions*).

The development of an honest self-assessment is one of many pendulums that have swung far and wide in the history of Christian spirituality. For centuries, it was not arrogance that crippled some Christians and infected wrong-headed expressions of piety. Instead, misunderstandings of the Christian message were influenced by a misguided view of humanity. In an effort to acknowledge the crippling power of sin, some Christians embraced some extreme notions of human depravity.

These notions were at odds with a healthy understanding of the human person as well as the nature of God's creation, grace, and redemption, which is a re-creation in Jesus Christ. Such distorted views can cause people who are spiritually sensitive to hate themselves, rather than help them to respond to Christ's call to appropriately deny themselves. A view of total human depravity fails to grasp the full beauty of the image of God present in all people. That image of God (in classical Latin, the *Imago Deo*) remains in each one of us, even though we are wounded, compromised, and marred by sin.

Such a mistaken notion of what it means to be humble still has its adherents and still needs to be addressed. Nowadays, however, another extreme swing of the pendulum has replaced it. Today's society participates in forms of self-worship that might well be identified as idolatry. This is all too evident, even in the Christian community.

> A VIEW OF TOTAL HUMAN DEPRAVITY FAILS TO GRASP THE FULL BEAUTY OF THE IMAGE OF GOD PRESENT IN ALL PEOPLE.

It is impossible for me to imagine that Jesus, if He were visibly present in the world today, would look, talk, or act like some of the more flamboyant characters in certain segments of the Christian media community. Would He strut across church stages, shout out slogans, tell us where we can find miracle money, or arrogantly mock others? Would He encourage us to "self-actualize," or to "manifest" a Mercedes-Benz?

In Mark 10, we read about a conversation between brothers James and John, sons of Zebedee, and Jesus. "Teacher," they said, "we want you to do for us whatever we ask."

"What do you want me to do for you?" He asked.

They replied, "Let one of us sit at your right and the other at your left in your glory."

This request for power and prestige was not an authentic prayer. "When the ten heard this, they became indignant at James and John. Jesus summoned them and said to them, 'You know that those who are recognized as rulers over the Gentiles lord it over them, and their great ones make their authority over them felt. But it shall not be so among you. Rather, whoever wishes to be great among you will be your servant; whoever wishes to be first among you will be the slave of all. For the Son of Man did not come to be served but to serve and to give his life as a ransom for many'" (Mark 10:41–45).

Jesus had just given a series of profound teachings on the kingdom, and as He and His disciples made their way through the countryside, He had invited one young man to sell all that he had if he was serious about following Him. Peter had pointed out that he and the other disciples had left everything to follow Him. Yet here we find the sons of Zebedee asking for a place of prominence for themselves. Why? Because they were still self-consumed. Notice their idea of prayer, "Teacher, we want you to do for us whatever we ask of you." Sound familiar? Then or now, living in humility is not about deciding what we want or intend to do, then asking God to bless it. Instead, it is about wholehearted surrender to God.

It is no wonder, presented with today's myriad contradictions to authentic spirituality and true faith, that a woman like Mother Teresa of Calcutta radiated such sacred luminosity. How we hunger to encounter genuinely spiritual people! And truly spiritual Christians are those who understand their lowly estate, but in the midst of it all abandon themselves fully and completely to a loving and merciful God who has imprinted His own image upon them. By seeking to know Him, they become like Him. They do not shout or strut. They do not insist on their own way. They defer—and refer—everyone they meet to the God they love.

> LIVING IN HUMILITY IS NOT ABOUT DECIDING WHAT WE WANT OR INTEND TO DO, THEN ASKING GOD TO BLESS IT. INSTEAD, IT IS ABOUT WHOLEHEARTED SURRENDER TO GOD.

The Virgin of Nazareth shines against this backdrop of human arrogance and the idolatry of self. We see her living a surrendered life of love. We recognize her as a prophetic sign for a waiting world. She did not promote herself; instead she cared only that all men and women should meet and be changed by her Son. She did not speak many words; she seemed never to call attention to herself. She lived entirely in love and for love.

Mary is still a model for our age and every other. Her self-deprecation did not reveal a poor self-image, but rather honest recognition of her smallness in the overshadowing presence of an infinite God. Any authentic spiritual life evidences this kind of honesty in self-assessment. As we allow God to look upon the "lowliness" of our own lives, we open the door for Him to come in, to live within us and through us. As it was with Mary, so it can be with us. Her Son still chooses to be born in the humble manger of every heart where room can be found for Him. Mary's honest self-appraisal is based not on self-righteousness but on humility. Humility was the way of her Son Jesus, the One of whom Saint Paul later wrote:

> Have among yourselves the same attitude that is
> also yours in Christ Jesus,
>> Who, though he was in the form of God,
>> did not regard equality with God something
>>> to be grasped.
>> Rather, he emptied himself,
>> taking the form of a slave,
>> coming in human likeness;
>> and found human in appearance,
>> he humbled himself,
>> becoming obedient to death,
>> even death on a cross.
>> Because of this, God greatly exalted him
>> and bestowed on him the name
>> that is above every name,

> that at the name of Jesus
> every knee should bend,
> of those in heaven and on earth and under
>   the earth,
> and every tongue confess that
> Jesus Christ is Lord,
> to the glory of God the Father. (Phil. 2:5–11)

The Greek word that is rendered in this text as "emptied" is *kenosis.* It literally means to be poured out as a drink offering. Mary accepted her role by pouring herself out for others. In so doing, she profoundly participated in the redemptive mission of her Son and Savior. The way of Mary is the way of self-emptying, for only in so doing can we be filled. Her way is that of taking the lowest place; it is the way of serving. Mary chose the path of becoming less so that her Son Jesus might become all in all.

The path to self-fulfillment does not lead to the accumulation of earthly goods. Nor is it found among the praises of other men and women. Nor does it offer to us the trappings and distractions of worldly power. We can only be personally fulfilled as Jesus taught us: The way to finding ourselves is through denying ourselves. The path to finding lasting treasure is through voluntary renunciation. That is Mary's Way. It is the way of her Son and Savior.

ONLY WHEN WE REALISTICALLY ASSESS OURSELVES, NEITHER WRONGLY DEMEANING NOR INFLATING OURSELVES, CAN WE BEGIN TO COOPERATE WITH GOD'S GRACE AND CULTIVATE TRUE HUMILITY.

Because of cruel verbal assaults throughout their lives, or poor religious instruction, some people believe themselves to be utterly worthless. Others have an inflated sense of self-worth and, unfortunately, a serious case of egoism. Mary had a balanced view of herself, an honest view; and she serves as an example to us. Only when we realistically assess ourselves, neither wrongly demeaning nor inflating ourselves, can we begin to cooperate with God's grace and cultivate true humility.

In the clamor and the glamor of our daily lives, may we empty ourselves of all else, so that we can be filled with Jesus Christ. May we find the grace to deny ourselves and choose the way of the Cross, and to thereby become God's instruments, upon which His song of salvation can be beautifully played. Our world has been filled with the cacophony of self, crying out in emptiness. May God help us to fully hear, instead, our Creator's symphony of love. May He grant us the grace to join in Mary's humble song.

CHAPTER NINE

EXPERIENCING THE JOY OF THE LORD

Behold, from now on will all ages call me blessed. (Luke 1:48)

M ary was the humblest of women, and yet she sang that all generations would call her blessed. In fact, her words were more than beautiful and inspired— they were prophetic. Over the centuries they have been proven true. In some Christian traditions, Mary is called the "Blessed Virgin," in others "our Blessed Mother." Christian believers know that Mary was chosen by God to be the first earthly home of the One who came to redeem the world. She was, indeed, "blessed among women."

The Greek word in the biblical text that is translated "blessed" is *makarios*. The word is more akin to a verb than an adjective; its tense is active, and it refers to a relationship. Those who recognize the sheer wonder of Mary's encounter with the Lord cannot fail to see the magnanimity of what God has done, for her and for the world, through the Incarnation. At its deepest level, Mary's blessedness refers to her relationship with the Lord who is the source of her joy. The Lord Himself calls her "blessed" by taking up residence within her and thereby inviting her into a relationship with Him.

Authentic joy and happiness flow from an intimate relationship with God—a relationship that He always initiates and to which we are always invited. Mary understood the invitation, responded freely with the surrender of selfless love, and now shows us the way to be happy. Her happiness truly is a matter of the heart.

In the choice she made during the angel's annunciation of

God's plan, Mary illuminated the path to true joy. Mary models for all of us what Saint Paul would call in his letter to the Corinthians "a more excellent way" (I Cor. 12:31). Love is the path to authentic joy. We are able to choose, as Mary did, a life-consuming, transforming relationship with Christ, who is love personified. When we say yes to God's offer, in a very real way Jesus is conceived in our hearts, and we are blessed, happy, and filled with joy.

> THE KIND OF HAPPINESS AND BLESSEDNESS GOD'S GRACE BESTOWS ON US IS NOT DEPENDENT ON OUR CIRCUMSTANCES.

The kind of happiness and blessedness God's grace bestows on us is not dependent on our circumstances. In a troubled and sin-sick world, we will inevitably encounter suffering. Mary certainly did. She was told she would be pierced with a sword (Luke 2:35), and she ultimately suffered nearly unimaginable grief. Yet her life, her losses, and the ordeal she endured—seeing her Son go to the cross—never eclipsed the blessedness she experienced. That same blessedness is available to us.

In the Eastern Christian tradition (Orthodox and Catholic) one of the most popular icons of Mary is called the *Platytera,* which means, "She who is more spacious than the heavens." It depicts Mary with Jesus within her womb, His arms outstretched for the world or, in some renderings, His right hand extending a blessing. In most Eastern iconography, Mary does not appear without Jesus. That is to emphasize the real source of her joy, the content of her mission, and the meaning of her life. God Incarnate took up residence within her for the love of the world.

To seek happiness or blessedness for its own sake is to reverse the proper priorities. Happiness is not a goal to be attained, but is instead a fruit borne in us by our participation in the life of grace. One of the happiest men I ever knew was a priest named Fr. Philip Bebie, who was my confessor and coun-selor at what was then called the College of Steubenville (now the Franciscan University of Steubenville) in Ohio. I first met Fr. Philip after he had accepted an invitation to build a small community of priests on campus. I, at the same time, had also accepted an invitation to build a small community of students, a "faith household," who would help foster spiritual renewal through prayer, witness, and common life. Having worked together in campus ministry, Fr. Philip and I remained lifelong friends.

After college, my marriage, and the birth of my children, Fr. Phil motivated me as a husband and father in my "vocation," as he rightly called Christian marriage and family.

Periodically, he would send me little reminders of God's love, and pictures of "his Lady," Mary, the mother of the Lord. He had a deep love for Jesus, and therefore also honored His mother. He also reminded me of the role that suffering, rightly understood, played in the call to holiness.

> TO SEEK HAPPINESS OR BLESSEDNESS FOR ITS OWN SAKE IS TO REVERSE THE PROPER PRIORITIES. HAPPINESS IS NOT A GOAL TO BE ATTAINED, BUT IS INSTEAD A FRUIT BORNE IN US BY OUR PARTICIPATION IN THE LIFE OF GRACE.

Before the end of his days, Fr. Philip himself personally shared in Christ's suffering. When word came to me that he was near death, I knew that I had to see him. I could not let him go without shar-ing one more talk, one more laugh, one more prayer, and one more hug. Immediately, I purchased an airline ticket. When I arrived, I drove the rental car through a dreary cold day, trying to contain the sorrow and fear that surged within me. I arrived at the huge Passionist monastery where Fr. Philip was staying, alone, in the infirmary. The huge facility—which in the 1950s had been home to over fifty men and even more seminarians—now housed seven old priests, including Philip.

I parked the car and approached the large glass entryway. Before I could reach for the bell, I saw a note taped to the door. It read, "Keith, I'm waiting for you on the inside. Fr. Philip." Eagerly awaiting my arrival was an old man with shriveled skin and a distended abdomen, but Fr. Philip's smile of intense joy lit up his piercing eyes, and a countenance of peace and joy animated his debilitated frame. He was genuinely happy. He was "blessed."

On his wall was a picture of Jesus and next to it a picture of His mother, Mary, the mother of the Lord, the woman for whom he had great affection. He spoke of both frequently over our remaining hours and encouraged me to discover the meaning and mystery revealed in Mary's *Magnificat*. Here was a man whose days and nights were no longer separate because of the intense pain. He was all alone in that infirmary, dying, but professing with great certainty that Jesus had been good to him. Fr. Philip was filled with a joy that I had never tasted.

He prayed with me repeatedly during our visit. He spoke the truth and reminded me of Jesus' promises. All too soon, it was time for me to leave. He heard my confession and pronounced absolution over me, laying his large hands on my head and praying that God's tender, fatherly love would continue to guide me. Seven days later, Philip went home to the Lord.

About a year after our visit, I was at home on a cold Saturday in autumn. The colorful foliage drew me outside, and I decided to take an afternoon walk in the brisk Steubenville air. It was getting rather cold, so I went up to the attic to get my blue wool overcoat out of storage. I walked through the woods, seemingly alone. Suddenly, I was overwhelmed with a sense of the presence of God's peace. I thought about Philip and how I missed him.

As I reviewed my life and responsibilities, I realized how much I still needed his counsel. I shoved my hands into my pockets to warm them, and felt a hole in one of the linings. That didn't surprise me. After all, this was an old coat—my favorite. But my fingers went beyond the hole to the inner lining and discovered a folded-up piece of paper. I pulled it out, opened it, and read, "Keith, I'm waiting for you on the inside. Fr. Philip."

He was with me still.

Fr. Philip responded to the God who is love crucified. In the words of his Master: "From the days of John the Baptist until now, the kingdom of heaven suffers violence, and the violent are taking it by force" (Matt. 11:12). Fr. Philip took it by force. He poured himself out in response to the One who had poured out His sacred blood for the whole of humanity. Fr. Philip, like Mary, was truly blessed. He sang her song. He pursued the same holiness in life that marked her life, and like her, he embraced eternity in love. He had said yes to God. He had conceived Christ in his heart, and made it his life's work to present Him to others.

I was one of many whose lives were changed forever because of encounters with Fr. Philip Bebie. His life demonstrated redemptive, sacrificial love. In him I witnessed the true blessedness that Mary sang about, the happiness that the Bible talks about, the inexplicable joy that Christians have experienced for centuries as they have walked along the way of the Cross.

CHAPTER TEN

ENCOUNTERING
REAL POWER

The Mighty One has done great things for me. (Luke 1:49)

The focus of Mary's prayer, Song, and her life was never on herself. Neither was it on the gifts she had received. That is why Mary revealed genuine spirituality. Her attention was always focused on the Giver of all gifts, the One whom she loved and to whom she surrendered herself completely. Her thoughts and actions proceeded from an intimate relationship with the One who created her in His image out of infinite love. She showed us how to respond to His grace in our own lives. In doing this, we can also experience a mighty God doing great things for us.

Immortal, invisible, infinite, and incomprehensible except through His revelation to humanity, God condescended to come among us as a baby. The Word, through whom the entire universe was made, became flesh and lived among us (John 1:1–14). The God who set the stars in their place, who formed humankind from dust, has made His home among us, and continues to be Immanuel—God with us—today. The incarnation of Jesus Christ reveals that true power is manifested in unconditional love, a love that gives itself away for others, a love that offers itself sacrificially, simply because of grace.

After Jesus' birth, the prophet Simeon proclaimed to Mary that she would be pierced with a sword (Luke 2:35). In essence, she was. Love suffers for the beloved. Mary knew God, and she surrendered to His Son in a fellowship of suffering. The early Christians also knew that the gospel call entails an invitation to join our sufferings to Christ's. Saint Paul wrote that he wanted to gain Christ, "to know him and the power of his resurrection and (the) sharing of his sufferings by being conformed to his death, if somehow I may attain the resurrection from the dead" (Phil. 3:10–11).

The Lord chose the path of suffering to make it possible for each of us to choose to live in full communion of love with Him. The redemption accomplished by Jesus Christ, because of His divinity, did what we as humans could never do. His agony, borne for love of each one of us, has opened the doors to the Father's house, and we are now invited inside. To know the Son, though, and to experience His power, we must also accept the invitation to participate in His continuing redemptive mission by sharing in His suffering.

The relationship between suffering and communion with God in Christ provides an insight into true prayer, genuine faith, and human flourishing. It is the beginning of an authentic spiritual power. Some speak freely about their one-on-one relationship with God, sounding at times as if Jesus were, in Frederick Buechner's words, "in their back pocket." These same people speak of God's Spirit as if they could control Him, even to the point of presuming that God's power will prevent suffering from coming into their lives. This is not the way of the Cross. It is not Mary's Way, nor is it the way in which Jesus leads each one of us. If we are to know Him and His power, we are also bound to share, at times, a measure of His suffering. This is, according to Saint Paul, one way of fellowshipping with Him. It is a part of the mystery of faith.

> IF WE ARE TO KNOW HIM AND HIS POWER, WE ARE ALSO BOUND TO SHARE, AT TIMES, A MEASURE OF HIS SUFFERING. THIS IS, ACCORDING TO SAINT PAUL, ONE WAY OF FELLOWSHIPPING WITH HIM. IT IS A PART OF THE MYSTERY OF FAITH.

As we see the mother of Jesus standing at the foot of the

cross, we should wonder just how painful for her the fellowship of His sufferings must have been. Christians have reflected upon her ordeal and its meaning for centuries. Mary's life demonstrated to us that when we share in the suffering of Jesus Christ, we will also experience His power and deliverance.

As I write this reflection I have just returned from the bedside of a wonderful friend. A man of only thirty-one years, he was thrown into a coma after experiencing severe dehydration due to excessive exercise. I joined his family, other clergy, and dozens of faithful friends in a vigil of prayer. In his short years this friend has touched hundreds with the love and joy of Jesus Christ. Even from a hospital bed in the intensive care unit he has continued to do so. Evangelicals, Protestants, Catholics, and Orthodox all gathered to pray. We knew that we prayed to the same Lord, and we discovered, at our friend's hospital bed, a path to a shared mission. His seemingly unnecessary suffering occasioned all of this. We will continue to pray for him, hoping to see God's power demonstrated in his complete recovery.

In her *Magnificat,* Mary exulted joyfully in having seen God's mighty power at work in her life. Today, two millennia later, it is not unusual for Christians to recount daily experiences of God's gracious activity. They tell their stories in awe, because they recognize that the power of God has touched them, doing for them what they couldn't possibly do for themselves. "The Lord has done great things for me," they tell you. They use the same words Mary spoke to her cousin Elizabeth, rejoicing in the power of God made manifest in her life.

Our modern world talks a lot about power—corporate power, political power, military power. Doubtless there is a place for these, rightly understood and ordered toward the person, the family, and the common good. But the ways of the Lord are mysterious. As an angel once revealed to a Hebrew prophet, the work of the Lord is accomplished "not by an army, nor by might, but by my spirit, says the LORD of hosts" (Zech. 4:6).

Our age also speaks of personal empowerment, of reaching our human potential, of focusing on our goals and letting nothing stand in the way of our accomplishments, and of using our human will to make our dreams come true. Thankfully, our Father in heaven knows what is best for His beloved children. We learn that His ways are above our ways, and when we surrender our personal goals, dreams, and power to Him, He is "able to accomplish far more than all we ask or imagine, by the power at work within us" (Eph. 3:20).

> THE KEY TO GOD'S POWER WORKING WITHIN US, AND AROUND US, IS SETTING OURSELVES ASIDE IN ORDER TO RECEIVE WHAT HE HAS FOR US.

The key to God's power working within us, and around us, is setting ourselves aside in order to receive what He has for us. Mary knew this. She probably had dreams—young girls often do—but when the angel spoke to her, she immediately set those dreams aside, along with any goals she may have set with regards to her future marriage to Joseph. She voluntarily laid down her human will, her rights, and her aspirations. She did this out of love and for love.

In response, Jesus Christ came and took up residence within her. "The Mighty One has done great things for me!" she exulted. And through her, because of her surrendered love, she has done great things for us. She points the way to the Mighty One, who still waits for us to empty ourselves so that He can fill us to overflowing with His power, His love, and His grace.

CHAPTER ELEVEN

RECOGNIZING GOD'S TRUE NATURE

Holy is his name. (Luke 1:49)

What did Mary mean when she sang, "Holy is his name"? Why would she say that God's name is holy? In a biblical sense, the name of a person is more than a form of identification. In the ancient world, a name revealed a person's nature. Many times in the Bible we find God changing the names of people—Abram to Abraham, Sarai to Sarah, Jacob to Israel, Simon to Peter, Saul to Paul—once they responded to His invitation and encountered His grace. The change reflected both their new relationship with Him and their individual role in His ongoing plan for human redemption. When God changed someone's name, He marked a change within, a transformation of his or her way of life.

In a similar sense, each of us has been promised that we will one day receive a new name, a name that will identify us as a member of God's family. "To the victor," we read, "I shall give some of the hidden manna; I shall also give a white amulet upon which is inscribed a new name, which no one knows except the one who receives it" (Rev. 2:17). We will only be fully perfected, or completed, when we enter into the fullness of that communion in Christ. Then we will have become the unique creations that God always intended us to be.

When Mary sang, "Holy is his name," she understood that God is holy, and that He wants all of His children to be holy. God sent His Son, Jesus, into the world to make it possible for us to have a deep and intimate relationship with Him. Through that dynamic relationship of love, He changes us into the holy women and men He wants us to become. Jesus said, "Blessed are the clean of heart, for they will see God" (Matt. 5:8).

In Christ's sacred humanity we have seen the eternal God. We have also seen, modeled by Him, the way we are called to live our lives in the here and now. God's name speaks of His nature; He is a holy God, and His name reveals and communicates that holiness. Since we, too, are called to holiness, He has made it possible for us to grow into purity of heart by His grace.

As we have seen, holiness cannot be feigned or pretended. It is not about a facial expression, a look, or a vocabulary filled with pious words. It is not about imitating the best or about being the best. Holiness requires us to be in a relationship with the source of all holiness, God Himself. God is so holy that, under the rules of the old covenant, His name could not even be spoken. Yet today, because of what Jesus Christ did for us on the cross, we have been invited to call this all-holy God *Abba,* which is a term of affection for "Father."

The meaning of *holiness* as consecration—being set aside for God—is not so much a thing to do as much as it is an invitation into a new way of life. Holiness means that we are made "naturally supernatural" through conversion, which Saint Paul explained to the Christians in Corinth: "So whoever is in Christ is a new creation: the old things have passed away; behold, new things have come" (2 Cor. 5:17).

The holiness Paul described is not a static event but a dynamic process, a way of living our new lives in Christ. This new way of living is the way of love. When we declare with Mary, "Holy is his name," the reference point, and the source of the grace that makes us new, is God Himself. And God is love.

Saint John wrote,

> Beloved, let us love one another, because love
> is of God; everyone who loves is begotten by God

and knows God. Whoever is without love does not know God, for God is love. In this way the love of God was revealed to us: God sent his only Son into the world so that we might have life through him. (1 John 4:7–9)

Beloved, if God so loved us, we also must love one another. No one has ever seen God. Yet, if we love one another, God remains in us, and his love is brought to perfection in us. (1 John 4:11–12)

God is love, and whoever remains in love remains in God and God in him. In this is love brought to perfection among us, that we have confidence on the day of judgment because as he is, so are we in this world. (1 John 4:16–17)

The holiness of God is revealed in the very nature of His love. He emptied Himself for us. The God who fashioned the entire universe, who dwelt in inaccessible light, came to earth and lived among the creatures He had fashioned. He made Himself vulnerable, and He did so for us. "In this way the love of God was revealed to us: God sent his only Son into the world so that we might have life through him. In this is love: not that we have loved God, but that he loved us and sent his Son as expiation for our sins. Beloved, if God so loved us, we also must love one another. No one has ever seen God. Yet, if we love one another, God remains in us, and his love is brought to perfection in us" (1 John 4:9–12).

Perhaps the most poignant depiction of this love was also recorded by Jesus' beloved disciple, John, in his gospel. Before Jesus shared a final meal with His closest friends, before He stretched out His arms to embrace the entire world joining heaven to earth, He wrapped a towel around Himself and washed His disciples' feet. The Son of God, before whom all the nations would one day bend the knee, bent His human knee before the ones He had chosen as His ambassadors. God, incarnate in Jesus Christ, took up a basin, towel, and washcloth (John 13:1–11). In this beautiful encounter we behold divine love in service, pouring Himself out like water in a basin in order to make clean all who had been soiled by sin.

In the same gospel we read the continuation of the love story. After Jesus washed His disciples' feet, He inaugurated the great Eucharistic meal, giving Himself as food and drink to all who would journey with Him to the Father. He explained that the blessed bread and wine were, in reality, His broken body and shed blood. He invited them to bring the whole world along to the feast. The great invitation—a missionary work that will not end until He returns—continues even now, through the mission of the Christian Church in our day.

> THE SON OF GOD, BEFORE WHOM ALL THE NATIONS WOULD ONE DAY BEND THE KNEE, BENT HIS HUMAN KNEE BEFORE THE ONES HE HAD CHOSEN AS HIS AMBASSADORS.

Finally, the holy One took up His cross and climbed the hill called Golgotha. He freely took on Himself punishment and derision, agony and abandonment, on behalf of a world that was literally dying for true love and holiness. It was for us—for you and me, and for all humankind—that Jesus walked the *Via Dolorosa,* the way of suffering. Every last drop of blood and water flowed from His wounded side for you and for me. In the great culmination of His redemptive mission, He who knew no sin became sin in order to break its power over us so that we might become the very righteousness of God in Him (2 Cor. 5:21). He paid the debt of eternal justice. He defeated Satan and the final enemy, death. He began creation anew.

Every day, because of what He did for us, we can choose to begin again. We can make this mystery our own. No mere spectators in Christ's passion, we who bear the name *Christian* are invited to become participants. We are called to pick up the basin and towel and serve others, to offer food and drink to the hungry and thirsty, to take up our cross and follow our Lord in a life of holiness and love acted out in humility. And there is more. Not only are we to live in the suffering and sacrifice of the Cross, we are also invited to receive into ourselves the power that raised Jesus from the dead—power that can transform us into the image of a holy God.

Our faith and love are meant to be active and fruitful as we follow in the footsteps of the God who washes feet. We are invited to give away our lives, so that we can discover our new life—and our new name—in Him. As we allow His power to transform us from within, we are made holy, set aside for God's good pleasure, as His Son lives His life through us. "Holy is his name," Mary sang. And by His grace, we are called by that name.

> Mary the Virgin is found obedient, saying, "Behold Thy Handmaid O Lord; be it to me according to Thy word." But Eve was disobedient; for she obeyed not . . . As Eve by the speech of an angel was seduced, so as to flee God, transgressing His word, so also Mary received the good tidings by means of the Angel's speech, so as to bear God within her, being obedient to His word. And, though the one had disobeyed God, yet the other was drawn to obey God; that of the virgin Eve the Virgin Mary might become the advocate. And, as by a virgin the human race had been bound to death, by a virgin it is saved, the balance being preserved, a virgin's disobedience by a virgin's obedience.— Justin Martyr (A.D. 120–165)

CHAPTER TWELVE

LIVING UNDER
GOD'S MERCY

His mercy is from age to age to those who fear him. (Luke 1:50)

The mercy of God is at the heart of the Christian faith. Mercy forms a bridge between justice and love. Mercy lies at the very core of God's revelation of Himself through Jesus Christ.

In the Old Testament, two Hebrew words, *hesed* and *rahamin*, were predominantly used to express the meaning of God's mercy. *Hesed* connotes an attitude of profound, loving goodness that, when it exists between persons, is revealed in a relationship of unwavering, deep fidelity. It also means grace and love. *Hesed* has a masculine connotation of taking responsibility for the obligations and the object of one's love. God always acted with *hesed* toward Israel, even when she was unfaithful.

The second term, *rahamin,* describes the love of a mother (*rehem* is a mother's womb), that gratuitous love toward a child that is intuitive and includes a range of emotions: goodness, patience, understanding, readiness to forgive, and hope. These two expressions in Hebrew, among many others, help us grasp aspects of the multi-faceted mercy of God.

Mercy has a name. It is Jesus, the One who will save all of God's people from sin. God's merciful love, as expressed through Jesus Christ, is more powerful than death, more powerful than sin, and more powerful than the separation between man and God occasioned by sin. God's merciful love would conquer all of that once Christ's work was complete. The end of His work was to become a new beginning for us all, because of the mercy of God. From Mary's physical tabernacle, God's only begotten

Son was born, revealing the ultimate meaning of mercy-become-man.

In the Hebrew Scriptures, God expressed *hesed*, or merciful love, in His faithfulness to His chosen people, the Jews. Through Jesus, He manifested His mercy to all the nations. Saint Paul recalls God's faithfulness to His people in his letter to the Christians at Rome. God's relentless pursuit of Israel continued into the New Testament, but ultimately, it was extended to the whole world (Rom. 9:15–16, 23; 11:31–32; 15:9).

Throughout Scripture, people are seen as the undeserving recipients of God's merciful love. Saint Peter proclaimed in his first letter to the dispersed Christians, "Once you were not a people, but now you are God's people; once you had not received mercy, but now you have received mercy" (1 Peter 2:10 NRSV). The entire New Testament takes up this exposition of the path between justice and love. Mercy leads to a cross on the hill called Golgotha, and explodes from an empty tomb.

> MERCY LEADS TO A CROSS ON THE HILL CALLED GOLGOTHA, AND EXPLODES FROM AN EMPTY TOMB.

The gospel, the "good news," is both a message and a mission of mercy. The word *mercy* is used repeatedly to describe the very nature and work of God. It also becomes the way upon which followers of Jesus are called to walk. In the *Magna Carta* of the Christian life, Jesus' great Sermon on the Mount, we are called to live lives of mercy. Jesus promised, "Blessed are the merciful, for they will be shown mercy" (Matt. 5:7).

In the tradition of the Catholic and Orthodox Churches, Mary is spoken of as the Mother of Mercy. In her life, and in the lives of all those who manifest mercy to others, Christ is revealed as the balm, the healing source for all human misery. Outside of a relationship of love with God, people are in a miserable state, living in the shadow of pain, fear, loss, rejection, and ultimately, death. But God has come to meet us in our misery. In the open arms of His beloved Son He extends His mercy to the world in an embrace of redemptive love. Because of Jesus, in Jesus, and through Jesus, justice and truth now meet.

Mary said, "His mercy is on those who fear Him." God has extended a special invitation in which, when we respond, He extends His mercy to us. There is a decision embedded in Mary's words, however. His mercy is for women and men who live in the *fear* of the Lord. What does that really mean?

In Greek, *phobos* is the word that is translated as this "fear" or "awe" of God. This awe is intended to lead us to an active love for God that changes how we live our lives for others. If we know Him, our fear of God is not about terror. The angelic messenger told Mary, "Be not afraid." We are invited to live in this awe of God, not in human fear.

True, God is mighty and His justice can be experienced as "a terrible swift sword." His judgment is formidable upon those who reject His invitation of mercy. However, in the words of the beloved disciple John, God is love (1 John 4:8). "There is no fear in love, but perfect love drives out fear because fear has to do with punishment, and so one who fears is not yet perfect in love" (1 John 4:18).

Unfortunately, some Christians misunderstand this distinction between the "fear of the Lord" and human fear. Because of this, they tend to move to the opposite extreme. C. S. Lewis pithily described people who view God as a grandfatherly being, "a senile benevolence who, as they say, 'liked to see young people enjoying themselves' and whose plan for the universe was simply that it might be truly be said at the end of each day, 'a good time was had by all'" (*Problem of Pain*, Chapter 3). This kind of god is variously imagined as a wish-granter, a cosmic butler, or some other benign force whose primary function is to make everybody's wildest dreams come true. Such views of the true God are both false and idolatrous.

The fear of God that we are invited to embrace—the fear that opens us to receive, perceive, and then give mercy—is an awe-filled reverence of who God is. It is an awareness of God's power, and a brutally honest recognition of our weakness; of His purity and our wounded and flawed nature; of His wisdom and our foolishness. A well-known proverb tells us, "The beginning of wisdom is the fear of the LORD" (Prov. 9:10). In Mary's words we find a deeper truth—the fear of God is also the beginning of mercy. When we fear God and welcome His Son into our lives, He extends His mercy to us in a life-transforming, redemptive, and fruitful relationship. We experience mercy, but even more, we become merciful ourselves, carrying His loving message to the entire human race.

> THIS KIND OF GOD IS VARIOUSLY IMAGINED AS A WISH-GRANTER, A COSMIC BUTLER, OR SOME OTHER BENIGN FORCE WHOSE PRIMARY FUNCTION IS TO MAKE EVERYBODY'S WILDEST DREAMS COME TRUE. SUCH VIEWS OF THE TRUE GOD ARE BOTH FALSE AND IDOLATROUS.

All who follow Jesus are invited to be messengers and mirrors of mercy. We are called to love one another as He has loved us—with a love that is, by nature, rich in mercy. He has taught us not to judge one another, and that is a form of mercy. He has modeled for us and instructed us to turn the other cheek, to go the extra mile, and to give away the shirt off our back. These are all expressions of mercy.

We see this mercy reflected in the life of Mary. As a mother, of course, she loved Jesus as tenderly as any mother would love her son. In later years, as His ministry intensified, Mary's faithful presence in Jesus' life became a profound expression both of her fear of God and of the mercy that is the perfection and manifestation of faithful love.

At Cana, in the context of a wedding, a symbol of Christ's love for His bride, the Church (see Eph. 5), Mary turned everyone's eyes to her Son as He demonstrated God's mercy in the first of His many signs of the kingdom. She showed mercy in her concern for the wedding hosts; she showed even greater mercy to all who would ever need her Son's help, proclaiming, "Do whatever he tells you" (John 2:5).

Mary cared about Jesus' well-being not only in spiritual terms, but also physically and emotionally. On more than one occasion, she went to some place where He was ministering, inquiring about Him and expressing motherly concern for Him. And what greater message of mercy could Jesus have received than to look down from the cross and see His mother standing, weeping, watching, and loving? By then, at least for the moment, it seemed that even the Father had rejected Him.

In bearing and birthing; in participating in the life, death, and resurrection of her Son, who was and is the Son of the living God; Mary was chosen, prepared, and privileged to play a singular role in the great manifestation of mercy to a waiting world.

> WHAT GREATER MESSAGE OF MERCY COULD JESUS HAVE RECEIVED THAN TO LOOK DOWN FROM THE CROSS AND SEE HIS MOTHER STANDING, WEEPING, WATCHING, AND LOVING?

Today, in light of God's mercy to us, we are invited to demonstrate mercy toward one another. We have been forgiven, so we are to forgive. We have been healed, so we are to extend healing hands to the wounded world. We have had our real needs met, so we are to become the vehicle for others in need. Like Mary, we have been blessed beyond measure, beyond expectation, beyond what we could ask or even think. These blessings are all ours solely because of God's mercy. Jesus said, "Freely you have received, freely give" (Matt. 10:8 NIV).

Chapter Thirteen

Understanding
Authentic
Strength

He has shown might with his arm. (Luke 1:51)

The strength of God, His "arm," is revealed in the lives of all who place their hope in Him. If we will but acknowledge our own weakness, we will find ourselves able to rely on Him, and to stand in His strength. Throughout the Old Testament we find numerous references to the strong right arm of the Lord. As a Jewish woman, Mary would have known every one of those passages. In fact, she was very familiar with the Psalms and, along with Joseph, would have taught them to her Son, as did all faithful Jewish parents.

In times of concern, Mary surely recited the words of the psalmist David:

> You rooted out nations to plant them,
>   crushed peoples to make room for them.
> Not with their own swords did they conquer the land,
>   nor did their own arms bring victory;
> It was your right hand, your own arm,
>   the light of your face for you favored them.
>   (Ps. 44:2–3)

When filled with joy, she would have uttered the ancient praises of God:

> Sing a new song to the LORD,
>   who has done marvelous deeds,
> Whose right hand and holy arm
>   have won the victory. (Ps. 98:1)

The phrase "arm of the Lord" runs throughout the Old Testament literature. However, it was the words of the messianic prophet Isaiah that revealed that expression's most profound meaning:

> Who would believe what we have heard?
>> To whom has the arm of the LORD been
>> revealed?
> He grew up like a sapling before him,
>> like a shoot from the parched earth;
> There was in him no stately bearing to make us
>> look at him,
>> nor appearance that would attract us to him.
> He was spurned and avoided by men,
>> a man of suffering, accustomed to infirmity,
> One of those from whom men hide their faces,
>> spurned, and we held him in no esteem.
> Yet it was our infirmities that he bore,
>> our sufferings that he endured,
> While we thought of him as stricken,
>> as one smitten by God and afflicted.
> But he was pierced for our offenses,
>> crushed for our sins,
> Upon him was the chastisement that makes us
>> whole, by his stripes we were healed.
> We had all gone astray like sheep,
>> each following his own way;
> But the LORD laid upon him the guilt of us all.
> Though he was harshly treated, he submitted
>> and opened not his mouth;
> Like a lamb led to the slaughter
>> or a sheep before the shearers,
>> he was silent and opened not his mouth.

Oppressed and condemned, he was taken away, and
    who would have thought any more of his destiny?
When he was cut off from the land of the living,
    and smitten for the sin of his people,
A grave was assigned him among the wicked
    and a burial place with evildoers,
Though he had done no wrong
    nor spoken any falsehood.
(But the LORD was pleased
    to crush him in infirmity.)
If he gives his life as an offering for sin,
    he shall see his descendants in a long life,
    and the will of the LORD shall be accom-
    plished through him.
Because of his affliction
    he shall see the light in fullness of days;
Through his suffering, my servant shall justify many,
    and their guilt he shall bear.
Therefore I will give him his portion among the
    great, and he shall divide the spoils with the
    mighty,
Because he surrendered himself to death
    and was counted among the wicked;
And he shall take away the sins of many, and win
    pardon for their offenses. (Isa. 53:1–12)

The Son—the One whom Mary conceived by the Holy Spirit,
bore in a Bethlehem stable, instructed as a child, and followed as
the first disciple throughout His time on earth—fulfilled Isaiah's
prophetic proclamation. The "arm of the Lord" was revealed
through Jesus. In Him, the strength and reach of God's arm
exceeded the entire revelation of God's dealings with Israel.
This God, who revealed His transcendent might and power to

Israel, lived among us and embraced all the nations of the world in love.

In my home is a unique altar. It is a bookcase, and on it is prominently placed the *Lectionary* of the Church (which contains the Bible readings for the liturgy of each day). Also on those shelves are the books of the *Liturgy of the Hours*, a compilation of Scripture and readings arranged according to the church year. Along with other favorites, these special books not only guide my daily prayers, but also help unite my voice with the voices of millions of others who are praying throughout the world.

Over this altar hangs a cross, and off to the side is an icon of Mary carrying Jesus within her. Tucked under the Gospels is a crucifix that I have had for many years. In one of my family's many moves, Jesus' right arm was broken off. It now lies next to the crucifix. I see it every morning.

I remember the day that I found it that way. At first I was saddened, but I was then struck with the richness of the symbolism. I sensed that the Lord wanted me to know something more about the strength of His arm. He reminded me that we, as Christian believers, are now His right arm. We, His people, are called to embrace the world in His redemptive love.

Love is, after all, the real strength of God's arm. There is no greater power in all the world than love, for God is love. One of the great heroes of the undivided Christian Church, Bernard of Clairvaux, once wrote of God's love revealed in Jesus:

> Love is sufficient of itself, it gives pleasure by
> itself and because of itself. It is its own merit, its
> own reward. Love looks for no cause outside of
> itself, no effect beyond itself. I love because I love, I
> love that I may love. Love is a great thing so long as
> it continually returns to its fountainhead, flows back
> to its source, always drawing from there the water

which constantly replenishes it . . . The Bridegroom's love, or rather the love which is the Bridegroom, asks in return nothing but faithful love. Let the beloved then love in return. Should not a bride love, and above all, Love's bride? Could it be that Love not be loved?

Mary proclaimed in her *Magnificat* that God had shown great strength with His arm. As the years progressed she would come to grasp even more profoundly the depth of that revelation. It became clearer and clearer through the One who called her Mother—her Son and her Savior, Jesus Christ.

In the Incarnation, God Himself had human arms. Those arms embraced Mary. They hugged those who came into His service. They reached out loving hands to the blind, and to those suffering with leprosy and other diseases. They helped crippled people to their feet, and lifted the dead back into life. Most powerfully of all, Christ's arms were stretched out in voluntary love on Calvary's tree.

> SAINT PAUL "BOASTED" OF HIS WEAKNESS TO THE EARLY CHRISTIANS IN CORINTH IN ORDER TO GIVE THEM INSIGHTS INTO THE STRENGTH OF GOD'S ARM.

The right arm of Jesus is the same strong right arm spoken of in the Old Testament. He was nailed to a Roman cross on behalf of the whole human race. His terrible wounds brought us healing; His death gave us new life. This is the fullness of the revelation of true strength. This strength—the kind of strength that comes from surrender to God's love—is offered to all those who will pray, obey, and live as Mary did.

Saint Paul "boasted" of his weakness to the early Christians in Corinth in order to give them insights into the strength of

God's arm. He knew of his own frailties, and he knew that the right arm of the Lord was never too short to save (Isa. 59:1). It was the Lord who told Paul in prayer, "My grace is sufficient for you, for power is made perfect in weakness." And it was the Lord who inspired Paul to proclaim, "I will rather boast most gladly of my weaknesses, in order that the power of Christ may dwell with me. Therefore, I am content with weaknesses, insults, hardships, persecutions, and constraints, for the sake of Christ; for when I am weak, then I am strong" (2 Cor. 12:9–10).

So it is with all of us. Mary recognized her smallness and her weakness. She did not pretend before God. That is why God could reveal His strong right arm to her. And He will do the same for us, and for all who truly seek His strength and, above all else, His love.

CHAPTER FOURTEEN

STAYING ROOTED
IN REALITY

He has . . . dispersed the arrogant of mind and heart.
(Luke 1:51)

Human pride, which stands in opposition to godly humility, has traditionally been called the sin from which all others arise. Pride is sometimes referred to as vanity. The human heart is the sacred place where God wants to take up residence. Pride is the thief that steals that residence. Vanity is the fraud that substitutes self, and the worship of self, for pure worship and true love of God. Pride is born in the heart not surrendered. It causes the disunity of self as certainly as the pride of Babel caused the disunity of nations. In the Christian tradition of the seven deadly sins, pride is the most deadly of all.

Some forms of Christian spirituality are inauthentic because they, in a sense, baptize pride and give it religious-sounding justification. The pride of legalism, the pride of self-righteousness, the pride of self-aggrandizement, and the pride of outward appearance all lead to the error of the Pharisees. Their arrogance was an offense to Jesus. The same error is repeated among the overzealous in every age.

In profound contrast to human pride and arrogance stands the Virgin of Nazareth. After the Annunciation, when the angel invited her to be God's chosen vessel for the incarnation of His Son, and His plan for redeeming the world, Mary might well have felt a surge of self-importance. She might have decided to let her friends, relatives, and fellow villagers know a thing or two about her new role as God's favorite. Needless to say, she did not. Instead, her song of praise to God—her *Magnificat*—offered a lovely portrait of her unfailing humility. Mary is remembered for her humble spirit. This, as we have seen, is not based on her lack of self-esteem, but rather on her clear and reverent view of who God is.

Pride is the enemy of love. C. S. Lewis wrote, "According to Christian teachers, the essential vice, the utmost evil, is Pride. Unchastity, anger, greed, drunkenness, and all that, are mere fleabites in comparison: it was through Pride that the devil became the devil: Pride leads to every other vice: it is the complete anti-God state of mind."

> "PRIDE LEADS TO EVERY OTHER VICE: IT IS THE COMPLETE ANTI-GOD STATE OF MIND." —C. S. LEWIS

A proud mind does not, in fact cannot, remain neutral. Those who are filled with pride begin to put themselves in God's place, making pride a gateway to idolatry. The Catholic Catechism teaches, "Hatred of God comes from pride. It is contrary to the love of God, whose goodness it denies, and whom it presumes to curse as the one who forbids sins and inflicts punishments."

Eastern Christianity, Orthodox and Catholic, speaks of fear of God as its only antidote to pride. "A festival for the spiritual man," Saint Ephraim the Syrian writes, "is the observance of the divine commandments, and his consolation abstinence from evil. His pride is the fear of God, his real joy the day when the Heavenly King calls him to inherit His eternal riches." This passage from *The Desert Fathers* teaches that a life of humility before God is the call of all men and women.

Where does pride come from? Its root is in the imagination. Like other sins, our wrongdoing begins with wrong thinking. Evil is bred in our thoughts, where we plot against others, envisioning scenes that degrade or humiliate them in order to exalt ourselves. How often excursions into fantasy center on self-glorification! We long to be admired, applauded, and acclaimed.

We conceive of scenarios in which we are the center of attention. But Mary tells us that the proud of mind and heart will be scattered.

Who do we imagine ourselves to be? What kind of specific glory fills us with excitement and desire, and fuels our vanity and pride? Do we want to be heroic, intelligent, beautiful, famous, strong, seductive, eloquent, rich, or powerful? How do we see ourselves when we daydream? It's not that we leave God completely out of our imagination. We may instead think He is singing our praises along with everyone else.

> HOW DO WE SEE OURSELVES WHEN WE DAYDREAM? IT'S NOT THAT WE LEAVE GOD COMPLETELY OUT OF OUR IMAGINATION. WE MAY INSTEAD THINK HE IS SINGING OUR PRAISES ALONG WITH EVERYONE ELSE.

Saint Paul wrote two letters to the Christians in Corinth. Not unlike contemporary Westerners, the Corinthians were filled with the pride of their own achievements. Theirs was a successful city, one they believed had reached the heights of human vision and accomplishment. Saint Paul instructed the Christians of ancient Corinth to resist the sin of pride:

> For it is written:
> "I will destroy the wisdom of the wise, and the learning of the learned I will set aside."
> Where is the wise one? Where is the scribe? Where is the debater of this age? Has not God made the wisdom of the world foolish? For since in the wisdom of God the world did not come to know God through wisdom, it was the will of God through the foolishness of the proclamation to save those who have faith . . . For the foolishness of God is wiser than human wisdom, and the weakness

of God is stronger than human strength. (1 Cor.
1:19–21, 25)

The preaching of the early apostles epitomizes this reality.
How could eleven uneducated men, born and raised in a remote
corner of the ancient world, come up with the radical idea of a
life-transforming faith in which God dies for love? At the beginning of Jesus' ministry these men had probably never even been
in a city or public square. How could they think of setting out to
change the course of world history by transforming human
hearts, one at a time?

The disciples were initially fearful and timid men. When
Christ was arrested, every one of them fled, despite the profound words they had heard, the miracles they had seen, and the
continuous presence of the One with whom they had shared
their lives for three years. Adding insult to injury, Peter, who had
been their strongest leader apart from Jesus Himself, actually
denied ever having known Jesus of Nazareth.

The truth is that God's ways always turn the world's ways
upside down. The disciples could never have conceived of themselves being eloquent enough—through the power of the Holy
Spirit—to preach Christ's message in sophisticated cosmopoli-
tan centers such as Athens, Ephesus, and Rome. When times
were tough they could only foresee resuming their careers as
fishermen. How could they have envisioned themselves coura-
geously facing brutal and violent deaths for Jesus' sake? By the
end of the first century every one of them, except for Saint John
the beloved apostle, had lived sacrificially and died a martyr for
the sake of the gospel. Who could have imagined such a thing?

Mary, who had worked alongside these first disciples, had
not been deceived into thinking that she had somehow transformed herself into someone important and significant. She
knew who she was because she knew who God was. From the

beginning, she was emptied of self. She was humble. She was rooted in reality, because you cannot get more real than Jesus Himself. The world was created through Him, and the cosmos is grounded in Him. He is the Word made flesh who dwelt among us (John 1:1–4).

Mary knew this Word by name. She carried the Word-made-flesh within her, close to her heart, for nine months. She birthed Jesus in a stable, where He humbly entered into a world steeped in pride. He spent His last three years virtually home-less, with "nowhere to rest his head" (Luke 9:58), and was con-tinuously faced with rejection and threats. Finally, He suffered the Cross. And in doing so, He scattered the proud and lifted up the lowly.

That cross is still the place where Christ's followers are gath-ered, humbled and grateful to stand near Him, made into a new people by the blood and water that flows from His wounded side. There, we join Mary, the beloved disciple, John, and the extended family of the Lord. He bids us all to come to Him, for He is meek and lowly of heart. In Him we will find release from our yearnings for significance. We find repair for our sin-sick imaginations. We find rest for our souls.

An Orthodox brother writes,

> Where dwellest thou, O humble soul; and who liveth in thee; to what shall I liken thee?
>
> Thou burnest brightly, like the sun, and burnest not out; but with thy warmth thou warmest all.
>
> To thee belongeth the land of the meek, according to the word of the Lord.
>
> Thou art like unto a flowering garden, in the heart of which there is a splendid home, where the Lord doth love to abide.
>
> Thee do heaven and earth love.

Thee do the holy Apostles, Prophets, Hierarchs and Venerable love.

Thee do the Angels, Seraphim and Cherubim love . . .

Thee doth the Lord love and rejoice over. (The venerable Starets Siluan of Mount Athos)

CHAPTER FIFTEEN

LIVING IN THE KINGDOM

He has thrown down the rulers from their thrones but lifted up the lowly. (Luke 1:52)

When he saw the crowds, he went up the mountain, and after he had sat down, his disciples came to him. He began to teach them, saying:

> *"Blessed are the poor in spirit,*
>> *for theirs is the kingdom of heaven.*
> *Blessed are they who mourn,*
>> *for they will be comforted.*
> *Blessed are the meek,*
>> *for they will inherit the land.*
> *Blessed are they who hunger and thirst for righteousness,*
>> *for they will be satisfied.*
> *Blessed are the merciful,*
>> *for they will be shown mercy.*
> *Blessed are the clean of heart,*
>> *for they will see God." (Matt. 5:1–8)*

When Jesus gathered His disciples around Himself and taught them the lesson that we now call the Beatitudes, He was proclaiming for all time the principles of His kingdom, connecting the great needs of His people with the abundant spiritual blessings they would receive from His hand. These principles were revolutionary, setting the wisdom of the world on its head.

Not many years later, after Jesus' return to the Father in heaven, it was said of those same disciples that they "turned the world upside down" with their preaching (Acts 17:6 NKJV). Those men were, for the most part, local villagers with little formal education. They had never been known for their academic prowess or oratory skills. Yet through their message they changed the world.

The same can be said of Mary, the Virgin of Nazareth. With little fanfare and so few words, she also turned the world upside down. The mighty are still put down from their thrones by the lessons of her obedience, and by the work of the "fruit of [her] womb," Jesus (Luke 1:42). The kingdom of heaven is still overturning the world's kingdoms and making folly of the world's wisdom.

The word translated "kingdom" can also—and perhaps more accurately—be translated "reign." The reign of Jesus Christ brings comfort to mourners, inheritance to the meek, satisfaction to the spiritually hungry and thirsty, mercy to the merciful, and the richest of blessings to the poorest in spirit. Christ's reign raises up the helpless and brings down those who rely on worldly power. As we contemplate these things, we come to see that lowliness is loveliness to the Lord.

Mary understood this truth. She also understood the primacy

of being over doing. Her life was first, always, and forever about a relationship with God. She is not remembered for her many activities or for her great accomplishments. It was her humility, her selfless affection for the Lord that endeared her to Him. She had no throne to claim, no personal realm to protect. She only recognized one throne and one realm—the one belonging to the God who called her, redeemed her, and revealed Himself through her. She loved the King of kings, and understood that His kingdom is spread through those who walk in the ways of meekness, poverty of spirit, and humility. It is God's power we rely on, not our own.

Sometimes we are tempted to think that our personal efforts actually expand the kingdom. This is not true. We are simply invited to *participate* as Jesus continues His redemptive mission. He invites us into His work, but He does not need our help. He only asks that we empty ourselves of self in order to be filled with the grace that flows from Him. That grace transforms us, and those around us, as we cooperate with Him.

Mary is an example of that kind of self-emptying love. As we've seen before, this pouring out of self is perfectly revealed in Jesus Christ who emptied Himself and took the form of a servant (Phil. 2:7). We are still called to live that same way. The life of the kingdom, in fact, is not about us at all; it is all about Him. We need to leave our earthly thrones and become lowly. We need to relinquish our realms of control, lay down our personal rights, and become pilgrims longing for "a better homeland—a heavenly one" (Heb. 11:16).

This action of putting down the mighty and elevating the humble is at odds with the idolatry of power, control, and influence that has permeated our contemporary culture and unfortunately infected some of the religious expressions of our age. Mary's example does not conform to the spirit of the age, addiction to human power. Today, even the Christian religion can become a form of self-exaltation disguised as piety.

Last night, I turned on the television because I could not

sleep. I was reflecting on recent events, and trying to put the illness of a friend into some kind of perspective. As I listened to some of the contrived Christian formulas for health, wealth, and feigned happiness that were being broadcast, my thoughts returned to the life of Mary, the ministry of Jesus, and the way God has of turning our human weakness into His strength. We cannot be saved by our might, only by His mercy.

During my friend's illness, I had heard sincere Christians from various traditions insisting that his illness was some form of demonic attack. They were convinced that somehow the devil was trying to stop a talented young leader from doing his important work. However, every time someone around me saw the devil, I saw the cross. Every time someone "took authority," I felt drawn to plead for mercy. The refrain of Psalm 136 flooded my days and nights as I, with many others, stood watch. "His mercy endures forever," I cried in my heart (Ps. 136 NKJV).

When all was said and done, God's mercy triumphed over the adversity in my friend's life. It always does. There is real power in the kingdom to which we are called. We can rest assured that whatever diabolical plot the enemy of our souls may intend for our demise, God intends only for our good. He is able to use anything and everything to move forward the reign of Christ, the kingdom of our Lord. But this is only possible when we set aside our own strength, humble ourselves at the cross, and totally rely on Him.

Certainly on the dark, gray day when our Savior hung on that brutal instrument of torture, which the Roman Empire reserved for the worst criminals, it seemed that the defeat of God's kingdom had finally occurred. There were three crosses on that hill. On one cross hung a thief whose heart had grown cold as he bitterly focused on his suffering and helplessness. On another cross hung a thief who acknowledged his own guilt and sought the mercy of Christ. Then there was Jesus' cross, the altar of pure love, the place where heaven was joined to earth. God's mercy, manifested in His Son's death and resurrection, is still throwing down the rulers from their thrones but lifting up the lowly (Luke 1:52).

A very dear and holy Christian man called me when he found out about our mutual friend's sickness. He had just turned sixty-seven years old, and he was in poor health himself. He told me that he was going to spend the night in prayer, which he did. The next day, when he called for an update, he recounted to me his prayer. At three in the morning, he had cried out, "Lord, I have lived sixty-seven years. I have been an unfaithful sinner. However, you have showered the greatest of blessings upon me. Please, Lord, our friend is only thirty-one years old, and he has so much to give in your service. Lord, if it is possible, take me instead of him!"

I wept when I heard the offer because I knew the heart from which it came. I knew that it epitomized the spirit of the Beatitudes, expressing the kind of love that can turn the world upside down. I was able to tell this man that the mercy of God had prevailed, and that our young friend was recovering. I was able to thank him for the sincerity of his intercession—a prayer that demonstrated the love of the cross.

As we think about the ways of God, and the promises He has made to the poor in spirit, the meek, the merciful, and the pure in heart, our minds return to Mary. She continues to shine as our example. She, the first of the disciples, reminds us of God's way of lifting up the lowly. She deserves our gratitude. She deserves honor for her obedience. She deserves remembrance for her humility. But as Aelred of Rievaulx preached to his fellow monks in the twelfth century,

> If we praise her with our voice let us not insult her by our
> behavior. Let us not pretend to praise her but do so in
> very truth . . . Truly to praise the humility of Saint Mary
> is to do everything in our power to cultivate humility . . .
> Truly to praise her charity is to direct all our thoughts
> and energies to the perfect love of God and neighbor.

CHAPTER SIXTEEN

PARTICIPATING IN HEAVEN'S ECONOMY

The hungry he has filled with good things; the rich he has sent away empty. (Luke 1:53)

Mary lived in simplicity. Today, in prophetic contrast to our Western excess, her humble life reminds us that simplicity is a path to holiness, happiness, and freedom. Simplicity is not about the quantity of the goods of the earth we may possess. Jesus said, "For where your treasure is, there also will your heart be" (Matt. 6:21). The real question posed by the witness of godly simplicity concerns our relationship with the goods of the earth: Do we own them or do they own us? In truth, God owns them all, and we are simply His stewards.

Mary's simplicity stands in contrast to two mistaken notions that emerge in every age. They concern our relationship to our possessions, things that classical Christian thought refers to as the goods of the earth. At the one extreme is a misguided embrace of economic poverty in the name of a spirituality that sees wealth and material goods as somehow intrinsically evil. Although some believers are called to voluntarily embrace economic poverty as part of a vocation, most of us live in the material world of bills, possessions, and financial challenges. We are to do so with gratitude and freedom in the Lord.

Matter is not evil. How can it be so when Jesus' earthly body was formed of matter? To think so is to misunderstand His incarnation and the resurrection of the body, which will take place in a new heaven and a new earth. In his first letter, the beloved disciple John wrote: "We have come to know and to believe in the love God has for us. God is love, and whoever remains in love remains in God and God in him. In this is love brought to perfection among us, that we have confidence on the day of judgment because as he is, so are we in this world" (1 John 4:16–17).

Our relationship to this world should mirror that of God's Son whom we follow. One of the great theologians of the twentieth century, Hans Urs von Balthasar, wrote of the relationship with matter, in these profound words: "In Jesus Christ, God has engraved his name upon matter; he has inscribed it so deeply that it cannot be erased, for matter took him into its innermost self."

The other error is often manifested in what has been labeled the so-called prosperity gospel, which equates God's favor with economic wealth. It is based on a false equation that the more money we possess, the more spiritual power we have, and the more we can see that God favors us.

> MARY UNDERSTOOD THAT WHEN YOU HAVE THE LORD, YOU HAVE IT ALL. SHE LIVED IN THE HEAVENLY ECONOMY, AND IF WE CHOOSE, WE CAN LIVE THERE TOO.

Many of the Jews of Jesus' day believed that God's favor guaranteed wealth and prosperity. But Jesus' life told a very different story. He was born in a manger. As an adult He had "nowhere to rest his head" (Luke 9:58). He was raised in a simple home by a woman whose heart recognized true wealth. Remember the words that the angel spoke to Mary when she asked how it could be that she would bear the Messiah: "Nothing is impossible with God" (Luke 1:37 NIV). Mary understood that when you have the Lord, you have it all. She lived in the heavenly economy, and if we choose, we can live there too.

In rediscovering our proper relationship to the goods of the earth—neither utterly rejecting them, nor wholeheartedly craving them—we will find true freedom in Jesus Christ.

The witness of Mary's simplicity demonstrates the freedom

that comes from a relationship with the source of all good things, the Lord. Choosing to live in simplicity helps us to find freedom from materialistic idolatry, and clears the way for us to participate in the redemptive work of the One who still fills the hungry with good things. Money is not evil. Nor is it proof of God's blessing and favor—a view that insults Christians who struggle daily to survive. Both errors fall short of the truth and are rooted in a mistaken foundation. They are centered on self rather than God and others.

The apostle Paul wrote two letters to Timothy, a young disciple who had been placed in leadership over the Christian community at Ephesus, a city that was known for its wealth and luxury. Saint Paul, who had traveled there to plant a Christian church, knew that those new Christian believers would face certain dangers when dealing with wealth. He reminded Timothy:

> Indeed, religion with contentment is a great gain. For we brought nothing into the world, just as we shall not be able to take anything out of it. If we have food and clothing, we shall be content with that. Those who want to be rich are falling into temptation and into a trap and into many foolish and harmful desires, which plunge them into ruin and destruction. For the love of money is the root of all evils, and some people in their desire for it have strayed from the faith and have pierced themselves with many pains. But you, man of God, avoid all this. Instead, pursue righteousness, devotion, faith, love, patience, and gentleness. (1 Tim. 6:6–11)

How often have we have heard, "*Money* is the root of all evil"? That is not what the Apostle taught. The phrase "love of money" is important because it speaks to matters of the heart (1 Tim. 6:10).

When we love the goods of the earth more than the One who created them, we commit the sin of idolatry. A destitute person can be just as obsessed with money as a greedy hoarder. Mary helps us see that a life of simplicity is the antidote to any disordered view of earthly goods.

In another one of his letters, to the Christians in Philippi, Saint Paul further explained his own approach to material things: "I know indeed how to live in humble circumstances; I know also how to live with abundance. In every circumstance and in all things I have learned the secret of being well fed and of going hungry, of living in abundance and of being in need" (Phil. 4:12). Paul was free from the love of money.

The Gospels of Matthew, Mark, and Luke describe an encounter between Jesus and a wealthy young man. This man had faithfully followed the commandments since his youth, but Jesus told him his personal piety was not enough. He instructed the young man to give up his possessions and follow Him. We read that the man refused and went away sad because his possessions possessed him. Consider these sobering words:

> Then Jesus said to his disciples, "Amen, I say to you, it will be hard for one who is rich to enter the kingdom of heaven. Again I say to you, it is easier for a camel to pass through the eye of a needle than for one who is rich to enter the kingdom of God." When the disciples heard this, they were greatly astonished and said, "Who then can be saved?" Jesus looked at them and said, "For human beings this is impossible, but for God all things are possible." (Matt. 19:23–26)

Again, we are reminded of the angel's words, "Nothing is impossible with God" (Luke 1:37 NIV).

The disordered love of things is rampant in our day, and many people are being poisoned by it. Thankfully, in some evangelical Christian circles, we find a healthy resurgence of interest in the spiritual disciplines, providing an antidote to the errors of the prosperity gospel. Similarly, in the Catholic and Orthodox traditions, we have a resurgence of classical spirituality. The Virgin of Nazareth serves as a model for all believers in our age. Mary's treasure was always the One whom she carried in her womb, birthed for the world, and followed throughout her life.

When we begin to recognize our own poverty of spirit, we are able to live lives that are completely dependent upon Jesus, who is the Bread of Life. Only He can satisfy the hunger of the human heart. Only He can occupy the place within us that is to be reserved for worship and complete devotion. When we have Him, we have everything, even though we may possess nothing. When we come to see that everything in our lives is a gift to be given back to the Giver, we begin to understand the way of simplicity. Only then can the goods of the earth be fully entrusted to us by the Lord who is their Source. Only then do we discover the secret of heaven's economy: those who live in simplicity are the richest people on the earth. Jesus called them the poor in spirit. He promised them blessedness. He proclaimed that the kingdom of heaven belongs to them (Matt. 5:3).

CHAPTER SEVENTEEN

CONTINUING THE MISSION

He has helped Israel his servant, remembering his mercy, according to his promise to our fathers, to Abraham and to his descendants forever. (Luke 1:54–55)

This last portion of Mary's Song reminds us of the memory of God—the God who always keeps His word. When God enters into covenant with His people, He faithfully fulfills His promises to all generations. The eternal Father who invited Mary to participate in His plans for the world is a God who works through families. In fact, it is His ultimate desire to adopt the entire human race into a loving family relationship with Himself, through His Son, in the Holy Spirit, and with one another.

Saint Paul wrote to the Galatians, "But when the fullness of time had come, God sent his Son, born of a woman, born under the law, to ransom those under the law, so that we might receive adoption. As proof that you are children, God sent the spirit of his Son into our hearts, crying out, 'Abba, Father!'" (Gal. 4:4–6).

As a daughter of the old covenant, Mary grasped by faith its deepest meaning. Because of that, she was able to bring the new covenant to the world. She was truly a daughter of Abraham, whom the New Testament reminds us is the father of our faith (Rom. 4:16; James 2:21). Abraham's daughter Mary becomes mother to the new humanity, to all who are reborn in her Son. She ends her song with the memory of the old covenant between God and His ancient Hebrew people. She also reveals herself as a participant in the new covenant, which has been made available to all the nations of the world.

The mother of our Redeemer played an irreplaceable role in the Father's unfolding plan of salvation, and in the fulfillment of

His promise to the generations. As a faithful Jewish woman, Mary not only knew of the promise of deliverance through Israel's Messiah, but she also longed for that deliverance. The book of Genesis, the first book of the Bible, repeatedly uses the Hebrew word *toledot*. It can be translated "generations," and comes from the Hebrew root word for giving birth.

Throughout the Old Testament, God reveals a pattern of working through families, one generation after another. It is still so for those who truly understand the Jewish roots of the Christian faith, and through that faith we, too, are now among the progeny of Abraham. Mary was a daughter of God's covenant with Abraham, and bore its fulfillment in the Son, our Savior. The Son that Mary brought into the world has fulfilled all of God's promises to Abraham and his posterity: "All the communities of the earth shall find blessing in you" (Gen. 12:3). In the *Magnificat,* Mary sings her praise to this God who spoke to "our fathers" and still remembered His covenant. She sings out of pure joy, celebrating her unique role as mother to the new humanity who will be reborn in her Son. How amazed she was that the ancient prophecy was being fulfilled through her— a lowly and humble peasant girl from Nazareth.

> MARY NOT ONLY KNEW OF THE PROMISE OF DELIVERANCE THROUGH ISRAEL'S MESSIAH, BUT SHE ALSO LONGED FOR THAT DELIVERANCE.

Today, through the Son of God we are able to enter into the fulfillment of God's promise to the generations. We are joined to the *toledot,* the family of Jesus. His Church has become the new family of faith. Just as the people of the old covenant passed through the wall of water in the Red Sea, we are delivered from the bondage of sin as we pass through the waters of baptism. By dying with Jesus Christ and rising with Him into the newness of life, we are set free to live as a part of God's own family.

In the New Testament, we read this:

> Faith is the realization of what is hoped for and evidence of things not seen. Because of it the ancients were well attested . . . By faith Abraham obeyed when he was called to go out to a place that he was to receive as an inheritance; he went out, not knowing where he was to go. By faith he sojourned in the promised land as in a foreign country, dwelling in tents with Isaac and Jacob, heirs of the same promise; for he was looking forward to the city with foundations, whose architect and maker is God. By faith he received power to generate, even though he was past the normal age—and Sarah herself was sterile—for he thought that the one who had made the promise was trustworthy. So it was that there came forth from one man, himself as good as dead, descendants as numerous as the stars in the sky and as countless as the sands on the seashore. (Heb. 11:1–2, 8–12)

Mary played a profound role in this great heritage of faith. By faith she said yes to Jesus' announcement of the new covenant. By faith she was willing to bear the disgrace of being an unwed mother. By faith she faced an ever-increasing heartache as she saw her beloved Son moving closer and closer to Calvary. By faith she stood in the shadow of the cross, and like her forebear Abraham, "believed, hoping against hope" (Rom. 4:18).

Today, by faith, the story continues. Because of Mary's obedience and God's grace, we are now Abraham's posterity too. We are the *toledot* of Jesus Christ. Through the faith of her fathers, the Virgin of Nazareth took her place in God's plan to redeem the world. By faith, we continue her mission in bringing

God's Son to our children, and our grandchildren, and all who follow. With her, we remember the mercy of the Father—never-ending mercy that He continues to pour out upon all generations.

PART THREE

Mary's Way

Blessed are you among women; for among women on whose womb Eve, who was cursed, brought punishment, Mary, being blessed, rejoices, is honored, and is looked up to. And woman now is truly made through grace the Mother of the living, who had been by nature the mother of the dying ...

For into Eve, as yet a virgin, had crept the word which was the framer of death. Equally into a virgin was to be introduced the Word of God which was the builder up of life; that, by that sex had gone into perdition, by the same sex might be brought back to salvation. Eve had believed the serpent; Mary believed Gabriel; the fault which the one committed by believing, the other by believing has blotted out.

—Tertullian (A.D. 160–240)

Heaven feels awe of God, Angels tremble at Him, the creature sustains Him not; nature sufficeth not; and yet one maiden so takes, receives, entertains Him, as a guest within her breast, that, for the very hire of her home, and as the price of her womb, she asks, she obtains peace for the earth, glory for the heavens, salvation for the lost, life for the dead, a heavenly parentage for the earthly, the union of God Himself with human flesh.

—Saint Peter Chrysologus, Bishop of Ravenna
(A.D. 400–450)

Chapter Eighteen

THE PRESENTATION
A Family's Obedience

When eight days were completed for his circumcision, he was named Jesus, the name given him by the angel before he was conceived in the womb. When the days were completed for their purification according to the law of Moses, they took him up to Jerusalem to present him to the Lord, just as it is written in the law of the Lord, "Every male that opens the womb shall be consecrated to the Lord," and to offer the sacrifice of "a pair of turtledoves or two young pigeons," in accordance with the dictate in the law of the Lord. Now there was a man in Jerusalem whose name was Simeon. This man was righteous and devout, awaiting the consolation of Israel, and the holy Spirit was upon him. It had been revealed to him by the holy Spirit that he should not see death before he had seen the Messiah of the Lord. He came in the Spirit into the temple; and when the parents brought in the child Jesus to perform the custom of the law in regard to him, he took him into his arms and blessed God, saying:

> "Now, Master, you may let your servant go
> in peace, according to your word,
> for my eyes have seen your salvation,
> which you prepared in sight of all the peoples,
> a light for revelation to the Gentiles,
> and glory for your people Israel."

The child's father and mother were amazed at what was said about him; and Simeon blessed them and said to Mary his mother, "Behold, this child is destined for the fall and rise of many in Israel, and to be a sign that will be contradicted (and you yourself a sword will pierce) so that the thoughts of many hearts may be revealed." There was also a prophetess, Anna, the daughter of Phanuel, of the tribe of Asher. She was advanced in years, having lived seven years with her husband after her marriage, and then as a widow until she was eighty-four. She never left the temple, but worshiped night and day with fasting and prayer. And coming forward at that very time, she gave thanks to God and spoke about the child to all who were awaiting the redemption of Jerusalem. When they had fulfilled all the prescriptions of the law of the Lord, they returned to Galilee, to their own town of Nazareth. The child grew and became strong, filled with wisdom; and the favor of God was upon him. (Luke 2:21–40)

The presentation of Jesus in the temple is a story of obedience, a study in the blessings that follow loving surrender to God in the lives of the faithful. God invites and deserves obedience. Yet in God's economy, freedom always accompanies obedience: We must *choose* to obey. When we do, we pave the path to our own transformation.

Even though obedience to His Word is what God expects of us, our voluntary response of obedience opens the channels for blessing, removes blockages to His work in our lives, and prepares the way for the fulfillment of His plans for each one of us. Obedience to God and His ways invites Him to bring our past, present, and future together. The choice is always ours.

God is love, and love never coerces. As a Father, God wants His sons and daughters to respond to His invitation of love and to the urging of grace. Saint Paul reminded the Christians at Rome that "all things work for good for those who love God" (Rom. 8:28). The same is true for each one of us. However, "those who love God" do so by choice. Love is the chosen path to obedience. Jesus said, "If you love me, you will keep my commandments" (John 14:15).

All those who appear in the story of Jesus' presentation at the temple loved God deeply. Every one of them kept His word faithfully and demonstrated that love.

Simeon and Anna, both of them elderly and devout, were blessed for their obedience by seeing the fulfillment of their past devotion. Through their encounter with Jesus that day, they witnessed for themselves the goodness of God and His unchanging

love for them. They knew that because they had been faithful to
Him, He had been faithful to them. Their God had kept the
promises He had spoken privately to them for many years. And
how they rejoiced!

Can you imagine the joy they must have felt in seeing the
infant, brought to the temple by His parents? Simeon came to
the temple that day in the Spirit. He was led by the Lord to see
with his own old eyes the answer to his prayers, and the fulfillment of his deepest longing—that the Messiah would come to
Israel before he died. Anna, after so many years of devotion, self-
sacrifice, and spiritual discipline, saw for herself the redemption
of Jerusalem brought before her by a young, unknown peasant
woman, accompanied by her working-class carpenter husband.

That husband, Joseph, was a son of Abraham who had
obeyed the words of the angel of the Lord. He "did as the angel
of the Lord commanded him" by taking Mary as his wife (Matt.
1:24). He had embraced the obedience of faith (Rom. 1:5; 16:26;
2 Cor. 10:5–6) and thereby became a part of the mystery of
redemption, hidden for ages in God's mind and plan.

This temple rite included a custom called the ransom of the
firstborn, which was an obligation of the father under the Law.
Joseph, the foster father of the Son of God, followed the
requirements of the Law. The *firstborn* represented Israel, the
covenant people who had been delivered or ransomed from slav-
ery in Egypt and now belonged wholly to God. At the temple in
Jerusalem, Joseph presented Jesus, who would become the true
ransom for the sins of the whole world, and through whom all of
the nations would be delivered (1 Cor. 6:20; 7:23; 1 Peter 1:19).
In doing this, he fulfilled the ancient Hebrew Law.

Joseph was a godly man who had seen more supernatural
activity in his life than he could have ever imagined. Now, once
again, he was hearing prophetic words—not only thanksgiving
for earlier prophecies fulfilled, but also predictions for the

future. It was his privilege to look beyond the dusty streets of Bethlehem and Nazareth and to glimpse evidence of an invisible world. Because of his obedience, Joseph's faith became sight. Luke's gospel tells us His "father and mother were amazed at what was said about him" (Luke 2:33).

In an even more profound way, Mary was blessed through obedience. From time to time over the previous year, she must have reflected on the angel's words to her. Her cousin Elizabeth had proclaimed, "Blessed are you who believed that what was spoken to you by the Lord would be fulfilled" (Luke 1:45). Now she was once again experiencing the fulfilled words of the Lord. She was standing in the Jerusalem temple with her promised Son, listening to His destiny foretold by old Simeon in haunting and mysterious words.

What she heard included predictions of pain and suffering. By allowing her to see what lay ahead, God was assuring her that it was all part of His plan, and that He would be with her. He would never leave her nor forsake her, no matter how rough the road. Ultimately, as with Simeon and Anna, all the joy and pain of Mary's lifetime would work together for good—not only at the Resurrection, but also at pentecost.

> JOSEPH WAS A GODLY MAN WHO HAD SEEN MORE SUPERNATURAL ACTIVITY IN HIS LIFE THAN HE COULD HAVE EVER IMAGINED. NOW, ONCE AGAIN, HE WAS HEARING PROPHETIC WORDS.

The child Jesus, too, was blessed by obedience. He benefited from His parents' faithfulness, and He willingly came under their authority. This example of obedience was the legacy He received from both Mary and Joseph. Mary had prepared Him as an infant, a toddler, a small child, and a young man. His thirty years at Nazareth informed and prepared His three years of public ministry, and led to the sacrificial conclusion of His life's work.

Joseph had taught Him the Torah, as any Jewish father would teach a son. He also taught Him to work with wood. Work was a daily expression of love for the family of Nazareth, just as it should be for us. In the workshop of Nazareth, Jesus transformed all human work into an offering of love to God.

In Nazareth, the life of this holy family became the first church, the domestic church. Through that transformation, we see the ordinary becoming extraordinary through obedience. Still today, when husbands, wives, parents, and children make the Christian home a place where Jesus is truly present, they become an integral part of the universal Church, Christ's body on earth.

Saint Irenaeus wrote, "God requests human obedience so that his love and his pity may have an opportunity of doing good to those who serve him diligently" (*Against Heresies*). The Christian family is God's first choice as a setting for the lessons of obedience to be learned. When faithful parents teach their children to obey their words, they also teach them to honor God and to respect His authority. They set their sons' and daughters' feet on a path of obedience, able to find their way into God's plan for their lives. By being raised in a home where God's Word was obeyed, Jesus was able to receive the earthly blessings that are the heavenly by-product of obedience.

How could we have lost him?
At twelve, a few were learning to hate their mothers,
Getting into trouble,
Running away from home.
But not this boy.
We smiled, knowing he was with the others
Until darkness fell, and no one had seen him.

Then pleasure turned to pain—again.

Three days, three nights,
The worst three days of my life,
Or so I believed at the time.
Was he dead?
Finally, in the Father's house,
Those kind but ageless eyes looked into mine.
"What did you expect?" he asked.

—*Lela Gilbert*

CHAPTER NINETEEN

IN THE TEMPLE
A Family's Transition

Each year his parents went to Jerusalem for the feast of Passover, and when he was twelve years old, they went up according to festival custom. After they had completed its days, as they were returning, the boy Jesus remained behind in Jerusalem, but his parents did not know it. Thinking that he was in the caravan, they journeyed for a day and looked for him among their relatives and acquaintances, but not finding him, they returned to Jerusalem to look for him. After three days they found him in the temple, sitting in the midst of the teachers, listening to them and asking them questions, and all who heard him were astounded at his understanding and his answers. When his parents saw him, they were astonished, and his mother said to him, "Son, why have you done this to us? Your father and I have been looking for you with great anxiety." And he said to them, "Why were you looking for me? Did you not know that I must be in my Father's house?" But they did not understand what he said to them. He went down with them and came to Nazareth, and was obedient to them; and his mother kept all these things in her heart. And Jesus advanced (in) wisdom and age and favor before God and man. (Luke 2:41—52)

Mary spent nine months carrying Jesus close to her heart. After His birth, she spent twelve years raising her Son, loving Him, teaching Him, protecting Him, feeding Him, and doing what mothers do—providing for His every need. Then, at an age when boys became men in most cultures, He revealed to her a deeper glimpse of Himself than she had ever seen before.

For several centuries the early Church struggled to define the nature of Christ. Was He divine with what only appeared to be a human body and nature? Was He human, but simply empowered by the Holy Spirit in a unique and special way?

Raging conflicts about the nature of Jesus Christ led to many of the first ecumenical councils in the early Church, and lay at the heart of several early schisms. When all was said and done, the church fathers concluded—by the inspiration of the Holy Spirit—that Jesus Christ was, in fact, the second person of the holy Trinity. He was both fully human and fully divine; true God and true man.

The first chapter of Saint John's gospel was, for centuries, recited at the conclusion of every liturgy. It was called the *Last Gospel,* and it plumbs the meaning and mystery of the incarnation of Jesus Christ, the second person of the Trinity:

> In the beginning was the Word,
>> and the Word was with God,
>> and the Word was God . . .
> And the Word became flesh

and made his dwelling among us,
and we saw his glory,
the glory as of the Father's only Son,
full of grace and truth. (John 1:1, 14)

The Creator of the universe, who dwelt in inaccessible light,
whom no man had ever seen and lived, became a real man and lived
among us. He became one of us. He felt as we felt. He laughed,
wept, feared, and experienced pain and suffering. In all this He was
tempted to sin, to make wrong choices, but He did not do so.

The claim that Jesus Christ is fully God and fully man has
been challenged throughout 2,000 years of Christian history. It
has withstood the assaults of heretics. It has helped to overcome
the fears of broken and wounded believers in every age. It has
made ordinary men and women into extraordinary saints. Even
today, the Word still becomes flesh in the lives of those who, like
Mary, say yes to God's invitation.

Created as a summary of faith by the undivided Christian
Church at the Council of Nicea, the ancient creed affirms,

We believe in one Lord, Jesus Christ, the only Son
of God,
eternally begotten of the Father,
God from God, Light from Light,
true God from true God,
begotten, not made,
of one Being with the Father.
Through him all things were made.
For us and for our salvation
he came down from heaven:
by the power of the Holy Spirit
he became incarnate from the Virgin Mary,
and was made man.

When Mary arrived at the temple that day, anxiously in search of her Son, none of this theological or christological framework had been refined. She was simply faced with what would have seemed like a rebellious episode from any other child. In fact, as far as Scripture reveals, it was Mary's first encounter not only with Jesus' growth from boy to man, but with His unique and singular nature as both fully God and fully man.

As a human child, He had shared a home with His mother Mary, and His foster father, Joseph, and had learned to assist in Joseph's carpentry. Now He had to be in His Father's house, learning His Father's business and revealing the wisdom of God to the elders of the temple.

The story of Jesus in the temple is not only a revelation of Jesus' divine nature, but it is also the story of a family in transition. It is the last time we see Joseph in the Gospel narratives. Church tradition seems to affirm that he died soon after, leaving Mary a widow. From then on, Jesus' role as the Son of Father God takes its primary place at the heart of the story and at the heart of His messianic mission. This change did not happen without pain. Even good change in our lives brings loss, and loss causes us to feel hurt. Mary, like all mothers, was seeing her Son grow up. And as she watched Him grow in "wisdom and age and favor before God and man," she must have felt the loss of her perfect baby, her delightful little boy, her wonderful child.

Suddenly, He turns His eyes on her in love, yes, but also with an authority and wisdom that she has never seen before.

As Jesus' role changed, so did the roles of those closest to Him. Nothing would ever again be the same in any of their lives. In the process, Mary saw, felt, knew, heard, and understood things that no mother has ever experienced before or since. Is it any wonder that she kept such things in her heart? The literal translation is "treasured" in her heart. Who but God Himself would really understand that treasury?

How kind to invite me, to include Jesus' new friends
      in the party;
We laughed and sang and danced until the wine
      ran out.

In the lull that followed, I told him what was wrong,
Never expecting such a curt response.
Embarrassed, not a little hurt.
Naturally, I chastised myself:
What did you expect? A miracle?
Nonetheless, I told them anyway, "Do whatever he says,"
Still hoping he would think of something.

I heard a quiet conversation, the pouring and splash-
      ing of water.
Then, wide-eyed, they stared at him in bewilderment:

      "Has there ever been wine like this?
      My God!"

                                        —*Lela Gilbert*

CHAPTER TWENTY

THE WEDDING
AT CANA
A Family's Dilemma

On the third day there was a wedding in Cana in Galilee, and the mother of Jesus was there. Jesus and his disciples were also invited to the wedding. When the wine ran short, the mother of Jesus said to him, "They have no wine." (And) Jesus said to her, "Woman, how does your concern affect me? My hour has not yet come." His mother said to the servers, "Do whatever he tells you." Now there were six stone water jars there for Jewish ceremonial washings, each holding twenty to thirty gallons. Jesus told them, "Fill the jars with water." So they filled them to the brim. Then he told them, "Draw some out now and take it to the headwaiter." So they took it. And when the headwaiter tasted the water that had become wine, without knowing where it came from (although the servers who had drawn the water knew), the headwaiter called the bridegroom and said to him, "Everyone serves good wine first, and then when people have drunk freely, an inferior one; but you have kept the good wine until now." Jesus did this as the beginning of his signs in Cana in Galilee and so revealed his glory, and his disciples began to believe in him. (John 2:1–11)

Next weekend I will attend my son's wedding. It is hard to believe that he is now a grown man, about to formally pledge his commitment to the woman he loves. Together, in the presence of the church, they will be invited into the vocation of Christian marriage and joined together. I anticipate the ceremony as well as the celebration. I know that I'll cry at the liturgy, and afterward will celebrate with great abandon, overjoyed at the promise of their married love and at the greater mystery of which it is a sign—Christ's love for His Church. And I will propose a toast to the bride and groom with wine, the symbol of celebration.

The wedding at Cana was also an event in which the solemn vows of a couple before God were followed by a celebration. Jesus and His disciples were in attendance, and "the mother of Jesus was there" (John 2:1). The scene at Cana revealed how the ordinary becomes extraordinary in the presence of Jesus Christ. Marriage is both a natural and a supernatural institution. Here we catch a glimpse of what theologians call the "nuptial mystery," in which Christ reveals His love for His Church. It is surely no accident that the first of Jesus' signs of the kingdom occurred at a wedding. It was at Cana that His public ministry began.

Weddings are extraordinary events. As a member of the clergy in my church, I have the privilege of witnessing many marriage vows. During the homily or sermon I always ask those who attend the same question, "Why do we cry at weddings?" I think the answer reveals something profoundly deep and extremely important. It helps us to understand who we are, who we are called to be in Jesus Christ, and the very meaning of human existence. Somehow, from a place deep within, we all intuitively know that weddings are a sign of hope and a prophecy of sorts about our own destiny. They reveal the plan of God for the whole human race. According to His Word, God desires to marry us.

Throughout Scripture, weddings and marriages are a symbolic framework through which the Lord speaks of His relationship with His people. He promises to espouse Israel to Himself. In the minor prophet Hosea's beautiful text we read,

> I will espouse you in fidelity,
>   and you shall know the LORD.
> On that day I will respond, says the LORD;
>   I will respond to the heavens,
>   and they shall respond to the earth. (Hos. 2:20–21)

However, as tender as the Old Testament allegory is, it pales in comparison to the deep beauty of the message throughout the New Testament. There, Jesus is revealed as the Bridegroom. He has called the Bride, His Church, to an eternal marriage.

This spousal union between the Son and His bride, the Church, was in the heart of the Father from the beginning. It was the "plan of the mystery" to which Saint Paul referred in his wonderful letter to the Christians at Ephesus (Eph. 1:10; 3:9).

Because of this, in the Catholic and Orthodox traditions, Christian marriage is a sacrament. This means that it both signifies and makes present the grace of God. According to the Christian gospel, all of those who respond to God's invitation of love, who choose to abide in Him, will live in His love forever. In fact, one of the final scenes in the Bible is "the wedding day of the Lamb" (Rev. 19:7–9). Here Jesus, the Lamb of God, is wed to His bride, the Church.

At Cana, we discover the foreshadowing of this event. The people have gathered, the party is under way, but then something happens. There is a dilemma. The wedding's host discovers that there is not enough wine for the guests. The bride's family will be embarrassed. The groom's family will be disgraced.

Mary was aware of the problem. The first thing she did was talk to Jesus. "They have no more wine," she told Him.

Jesus answered her in an unexpected way, reminiscent of His response at the temple. "Dear woman," He said, "why do you involve me? My time has not yet come."

At the temple, He pointed out that He belonged in His Father's house. Here we see that He is focused on His Father's work—the work the Father has given Jesus to do. Once again we see His divine nature. We know that God's ways are above our ways. Jesus does not see the lack of wine from the same perspective as the other guests. He sees it as far more than an unfortunate incident or a family disaster, marked in time and space.

> CHRISTIAN MARRIAGE IS A SACRAMENT. THIS MEANS THAT IT BOTH SIGNIFIES AND MAKES PRESENT THE GRACE OF GOD.

From Jesus' point of view, the Cana wedding is part of an unfolding eternal story. Yes, the wine had run out. But in the wisdom of God's Son, it was not a dilemma at all. In reality, the best wine had been saved for the last.

Did Mary know what was about to happen? Did she foresee the miracle? Or did she simply know that Jesus could be trusted, counted on to help the distraught banquet-master? In any case, she knew her Son. And her words at Cana offer us the wisdom of a lifetime and the path to eternity, no matter what dilemma we may be facing. She hears her Son's reply, then returns to the banquet-master and simply says, "Do whatever He tells you."

Her words reflected her own way of life, which was completely surrendered to her Son, her Savior, and Lord. In her few words, she also calls us to surrender to Him in faith and obedience. By listening to what Jesus says, we profess our trust in Him; by doing what He says to do, we choose to obey in love the One who is love incarnate.

> SHE HEARS HER SON'S REPLY, THEN RETURNS TO THE BANQUET-MASTER AND SIMPLY SAYS, "DO WHATEVER HE TELLS YOU." HER WORDS REFLECTED HER OWN WAY OF LIFE, WHICH WAS COMPLETELY SURRENDERED TO HER SON, HER SAVIOR, AND LORD.

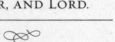

On a sheer human level, wine is a vital part of a celebration. There is no doubt that wine was an integral part of the Jewish lifestyle and that its consumption as a part of celebration was good, a sign of God's favor. The psalmist writes of the Lord,

> You raise grass for the cattle
> and plants for our beasts of burden.
> You bring bread from the earth,
> and wine to gladden our hearts,
> Oil to make our faces gleam,
> food to build our strength. (Ps. 104:14–15)

By turning water into wine, Jesus made it possible for a very human and joyful celebration to continue. I have no doubt that He also partook of the wine, and that Mary did too. But there is so much more to this first sign, this encounter with the power of the kingdom of God revealed at Cana. Wine is a symbol of God's covenant. The Jews use it as a part of the Seder meal and the Passover. At the Last Supper, it became part of the Eucharist, the heart of Christian worship.

Of the Communion wine, Saint Paul wrote, "The cup of blessing that we bless, is it not a participation in the blood of Christ? The bread that we break, is it not a participation in the body of Christ?" (I Cor. 10:16). Jesus had spoken of the mystery of that meal: "I say to you, unless you eat the flesh of the Son of Man and drink his blood, you do not have life within you. Whoever eats my flesh and drinks my blood has eternal life, and I will raise him on the last day. For my flesh is true food, and my blood is true drink" (John 6:53–55).

Here at Jesus' first sign, Mary's motherly request revealed her confidence in her Son, and her willingness to intercede with Him on behalf of others. Jesus' response to her, not only in words but in the performance of His first recorded miracle, discloses His nature—fully human and fully divine. At Cana, Jesus honored His earthly mother. He also revealed His heavenly Father's glory.

The air trembles with unfamiliar sounds
And dark fears, darker than the moonless sky,
Colder than the black wind.

Where is he, Lord?
My beloved son—is he warm and asleep
Or sleepless, stretched across some stony patch of earth?
And why, Lord?
Why not here?
Here he could be safe,
            Cherished,
                  Sheltered from the vulgar, filthy crowds,
            From those priests of Yours
Who watch his every move.

You give sleep to Your beloved,
But is he asleep?
Are You?
Forgive me, God.
But no mother could close her eyes on such a night.

—Lela Gilbert

CHAPTER TWENTY-ONE

WHO IS MY MOTHER?
The Family Defined

(Someone told him, "Your mother and your brothers are standing outside, asking to speak with you.") But he said in reply to the one who told him, "Who is my mother? Who are my brothers?" And stretching out his hand toward his disciples, he said, "Here are my mother and my brothers. For whoever does the will of my heavenly Father is my brother, and sister, and mother." (Matt. 12:47–50)

I t must have been a startling moment. Jesus, who epitomized the grace of God, glanced at the woman who had
loved Him all His life, cared for Him, nurtured Him,
taught Him God's way, and prayed for Him. Then He said,
"Who is my mother?" The words were shocking, perhaps even a
little hard to hear.

Some have claimed that this passage from Saint Matthew's
gospel implies that Jesus was lessening the importance of His
earthly mother. In fact, it has unfortunately been used as a polemic
to attack any importance given to Mary in God's plan of salvation.
Such a reading not only wrongly ascribes a minimalist role to Mary
in the Christian revelation, but also misses a profound truth con-
cerning the Christian life and vocation. Why? Because when Jesus
said, "Who is my mother?" He wasn't finished.

"Here are my mother and my brothers," He went on, probably gesturing with a sweep of His hand across the crowd to
indicate that His words included all who were listening and
learning from Him. "For whoever does the will of my heavenly
Father is my brother, and sister, and mother."

Jesus was not trivializing His relationship with Mary. He was
not insulting her. He was not rejecting His human birth mother,
and thus His human nature. Instead, Jesus was defining a new
kind of family. We know that as a man, Jesus' family was limited
by the bloodlines and intermarriages that exist in every family.
We see evidence of this in the genealogies recorded in Matthew 1
and Luke 3. Jesus was an earthly man with an earthly family.

But Jesus was, as we've seen, fully man and fully God. And Jesus' divine family is much larger indeed. With words spoken to a stranger in the crowd, He embraced into His family circle all who love Him, believe in Him, and do His will. We are the family of God. Through our baptism we actually enter into communion with the holy Trinity. Every Christian is part of the family of God. Through our second, spiritual birth (John 3:4–16) we become mother, sister, and brother to the Lord.

Mary is, of course, Jesus' birth mother. He was conceived in her womb, and brought into the world through her. But Mary was also, by faith, part of His heavenly family. Our great family of God, the Church, the communion of all saints—living and dead and yet to be born—is comprised of all who ever have or ever will enter into a relationship with God, in and through Jesus Christ, and be born into the Church through the waters of baptism.

> THE CHRISTIAN CHURCH IS NOT *JUST LIKE* A FAMILY. THROUGH THE REDEMPTIVE WORK OF JESUS CHRIST, THE CHURCH *IS* A FAMILY.

The new family that Jesus came to bring into being, the family of which He is the Head, is a real, tangible community. It involves authentic, diverse relationships, all of which are transformed by Jesus Christ from time into eternity. These relationships touch upon, model, and make present an eternal mystery—conceived for our good in the heart of the Father. The Christian Church is not *just like* a family. Through the redemptive work of Jesus Christ, the Church *is* a family.

Jesus defines this family not by race, color, or creed but by something far subtler: "Whoever does the will of my heavenly Father." And what is His Father's will? We have seen that by humbling ourselves, by obeying God's Word, by placing our faith in Him, and at times by even sharing in His suffering, we come into a family relationship with Jesus. Saint Paul added another dimension when he said, "See that no one returns evil for evil; rather, always seek what is good (both) for each other and for all. Rejoice always. Pray without ceasing. In all circumstances give thanks, for this is the will of God for you in Christ Jesus" (1 Thess. 5:15–18).

"Finding the will of God" is occasionally the subject of debate, conjecture, and opining among Christians. Some, with a wry smile, ask how such an important thing as God's will could possibly be lost. Others sign up for seminars, read books and essays, sit through lectures, and follow an assortment of keys and action items in search of this elusive goal. They seem to want to crack open some heavenly fortune cookie and read the mysterious message— "God's perfect will"—that is hidden inside.

> IT IS JESUS' WILL FOR US TO TAKE UP OUR CROSS AND FOLLOW HIM. WHEN WE DO SO, WITH A SWEEP OF HIS HAND, HE INCLUDES US AS MEMBERS OF HIS GREAT AND ETERNAL FAMILY.

In reality, although God's will for our personal future, including career, marriage partner, and other pursuits is rarely revealed in advance, God's will for our daily lives is not difficult to discover. God simply wants us to surrender our human will to His. Saint Thomas of Aquinas wrote extensively about will, both human and divine, and succinctly summed it up saying, "To give one's will to God is to give all."

It was the will of the Father for Jesus to give up His heavenly home and to offer up His life for humankind on the cross.

It is Jesus' will for us to take up our cross and follow Him. When we do so, with a sweep of His hand, He includes us as members of His great and eternal family. Saint Paul wrote, "Blessed be the God and Father of our Lord Jesus Christ, who has blessed us in Christ with every spiritual blessing in the heavens, as he chose us in him, before the foundation of the world, to be holy and without blemish before him. In love he destined us for adoption to himself through Jesus Christ, in accord with the favor of his will" (Eph. 1:3–5). It is God's will for us to be adopted into His family.

Through Jesus' life, death, and resurrection, creation has begun anew. He has opened the way for every man, woman, and child to enter into His family circle. Heaven has come to earth so that we who are of the earth might become heavenly. Once slaves, chained and captive under the bondage of sin, we are now set free to become the sons and daughters of the living God. Along with Mary, and all the saints, we have unlimited access to our Father through the work of His Son—our Brother—Jesus Christ.

CHAPTER TWENTY-TWO

AT THE CROSS
The Family Enlarged

Standing by the cross of Jesus were his mother and his mother's sister, Mary the wife of Clopas, and Mary of Magdala. When Jesus saw his mother and the disciple there whom he loved, he said to his mother, "Woman, behold, your son." Then he said to the disciple, "Behold, your mother." And from that hour the disciple took her into his home. (John 19:25–27)

STABAT MATER DOLOROSA

At the Cross, her station keeping,
Stood the mournful Mother weeping,
Close to Jesus to the last:
Through her heart, His sorrow sharing,
All His bitter anguish bearing,
Now at length the sword had passed.
Oh, how sad and sore distressed
Was that Mother highly blest
Of the sole-begotten One!
Christ above in torment hangs;
She beneath beholds the pangs
Of her dying, glorious Son.
Is there one who would not weep,
Whelmed in miseries so deep,
Christ's dear Mother to behold?
Can the human heart refrain
From partaking in her pain,
In that Mother's pain untold?
Bruised, derided, cursed, defiled,
She beheld her tender Child,
All with bloody scourges rent;
For the sins of His own nation,
Saw Him hang in desolation,
Till His Spirit forth He sent.
—*attributed to Bernard of Clairvaux*

Sometimes, when we approach the Cross, we approach it in horror, grief, and helplessness. Looking back across two millennia, we still cannot comprehend what we see there—the blood, the sounds of agony, the mocking crowd. And we are somehow amazed to find the mother of Jesus standing nearby, in the company of Saint John and a handful of others. How can she bear to watch her Son suffering a torturous death, dying by inches as the life ebbs out of His crushed body? And yet how can she leave? How can she turn her back and walk away? Where would she go? What can she do but stand and watch?

There is no record of Mary having spoken a word during those bitter hours. She was not a woman of many words anyway, and there was nothing she could say. Perhaps, as she stood there, she remembered the moments of Jesus' life that she had kept in her heart—His birth, the visit of the Magi, the flight into Egypt. Maybe she was remembering the conversation in the temple with Simeon, in which she was told that a sword would pierce her. Surely that day had come. Her own physical death could not have been more painful.

She may have reflected on the wedding at Cana, when Jesus said, "Dear woman, why do you involve me? My time has not yet come." Well, His time had certainly come that Friday. And now the faithful woman who had keenly felt His new life begin in Bethlehem stood and watched it end on a bleak hillside outside Jerusalem's city wall. Just as the water-made-wine had flowed freely into the chalices of the wedding guests at Cana, as she looked on, the blood and water flowed from His side, spilling into crimson pools on the earth.

"Woman," He had called her at Cana. Just then she heard His voice again.

"Woman," He began, fighting for every breath, fixing His eyes on her, then on John, "behold, your son." Then He said to John, "Behold, your mother."

Within the hour, we read, John took her away from that brutal scene, and made a home for her with him from that day on.

In the gospel story, Jesus had already defined the family. On the day His mother and brothers had gone looking for Him, as we've seen, He had given a heavenly dimension to the earthly family by including all who do the will of His Father as His mother, brothers, and sisters. Now, with His last breath, He gives His mother to John. In doing so, He symbolically makes her the mother of all believers. "And from that hour the disciple took her into his home."

> "WOMAN," HE BEGAN, FIGHTING FOR EVERY BREATH, FIXING HIS EYES ON HER, THEN ON JOHN, "BEHOLD, YOUR SON." THEN HE SAID TO JOHN, "BEHOLD, YOUR MOTHER."

Here is an interesting question. Have we taken Mary into our homes? Have we, like John, included her in our families? Because of misunderstanding, mistakes, and misinterpretation, Mary is often rejected by protestant Christians. Some say, "She doesn't deserve any more honor than any other woman." She is rejected as a symptom of paganism, or an indication of idolatry, or even a revival of some ancient mothergoddess cult. Mostly, this is rooted in a lack of knowledge or inherited generations of suspicion rooted in the divisions within the Church, brought about by our own sins against unity.

Yet Mary was called in the Scripture, "blessed among women." She was said to be "full of grace." Martin Luther wrote in 1529, "Mary is the Mother of Jesus and the Mother of us all. If Christ be ours . . . all that he has must be ours, and His Mother also must be ours."

How do we include Mary into our lives? We do so by walking in her way. It is the way of humility, obedience, and faith. Here we see that she, too, followed the way of the Cross. Jesus was wounded for our transgressions. Mary's heart was wounded for Jesus. She was broken by her love for Him. She received salvation through His death; she received new life through His resurrection; and as we will see in the next chapter, she received the Holy Spirit with the other disciples in the Upper Room on Pentecost Sunday. Surely she is our sister. But she is more.

Are we afraid to respond to Jesus' words to John at the cross: "Behold, your mother"?

Mary's Way leads us to Calvary, and from there to the empty tomb. It is not an easy path, but Mary was unafraid. By her faithful and humble life, and by her presence at the cross, she shows us how to overcome the greatest obstacle to the spiritual life, fear. Let us meet her in her pain, her loss, and her grief. Let us choose, then, without fear, to accept suffering into our lives as she did, to welcome the wounds of love. Only in doing so can we also share with her the joy of the Resurrection.

A wonderful Western abbot named Columban once instructed his monks on the Christian life in a writing that contains these words of prayer:

> Inspire our hearts I ask you Jesus, with that breath of your Spirit; wound our souls with your love, so that the soul of each and every one of us may say in truth: Show me my soul's desire, for I am wounded by love. These are the wounds I wish for Lord. Blessed is the soul so wounded by love. Such a soul seeks the fountain of eternal life and drinks

from it, although it continues to thirst and its thirst grows ever greater as it drinks. Therefore, the more the soul loves, the more it desires to love, and the greater its suffering, the greater its healing. In this same way our God and Lord Jesus Christ, the good and saving Physician, wound the depths of our souls with a healing wound—the same Jesus Christ who reigns in unity with the father and the Holy Spirit, forever and ever. Amen.

CHAPTER TWENTY-THREE

PENTECOST SUNDAY
The Family Empowered

When they entered the city they went to the upper room where they were staying, Peter and John and James and Andrew, Philip and Thomas, Bartholomew and Matthew, James son of Alphaeus, Simon the Zealot, and Judas son of James. All these devoted themselves with one accord to prayer, together with some women, and Mary the mother of Jesus, and his brothers. (Acts 1:13—14)

When the time for Pentecost was fulfilled, they were all in one place together. And suddenly there came from the sky a noise like a strong driving wind, and it filled the entire house in which they were. Then there appeared to them tongues as of fire, which parted and came to rest on each one of them. And they were all filled with the holy Spirit and began to speak in different tongues, as the Spirit enabled them to proclaim. (Acts 2:1—4)

It was a hopeful gathering of Jesus' friends that came together on Pentecost Sunday. Those who knew Him best were there, including His mother, Mary. All of them had walked with Him and talked with Him. Some of them had actually been at the cross, but every one of them knew in detail how that gruesome event had unfolded. They had all been stirred by rumors of the Resurrection; they had been present during some of His unannounced appearances. After the entombment, the silence, the depression, they had seen Him fully alive, had touched His warm flesh, and yet had perceived that He was somehow changed.

Before He returned to heaven, Jesus had instructed them to expect the arrival of His Spirit. He had spoken a great deal about the Comforter, the Spirit of Truth who would come. He had promised, "He will guide you to all truth. He will not speak on his own, but He will speak what he hears, and will declare to you the things that are coming. He will glorify me" (John 16:13–14).

So now they waited. Everything He had foretold about His death and return to life had happened just as He said. Surely this would too.

They had gathered in one place, joined together for one purpose, when, all at once, the promise of Jesus was fulfilled. He had told them that He must ascend, in His own words, to "my Father and your Father, to my God and your God" (John 20:17) because "if I do not go, the Advocate will not come to you" (John 16:7).

But did they know what to expect? Did they anticipate the

supernatural sound, the mighty wind, the flames of fire? Mary had spoken face-to-face with the angel Gabriel, given birth to God's Son while remaining a virgin, and watched as Jesus performed countless miracles. She had seen Him die, live again, and ascend into heaven. Perhaps she wondered what could possibly happen next.

Suddenly, as they waited, the Holy Spirit was poured out upon those first believers, and through them, upon the Church. In an indescribable moment, Jesus sent His Spirit to empower His new family. The men and women in the Upper Room were equipped to live as a new people, constituted in history, and called to lead the world back to the Father through the Son. Now the third person of the Trinity presided over them, filling them with the fiery, energizing life of the living God.

Through the Holy Spirit, those believers were now able to continue in uninterrupted communion with Jesus, and through Jesus, with the Father. They were *in Jesus* with one another. Jesus was *in them* for the sake of the world.

Following pentecost,

> They devoted themselves to the teaching of the apostles and to the communal life, to the breaking of the bread and to the prayers. Awe came upon everyone, and many wonders and signs were done through the apostles. All who believed were together and had all things in common; they would sell their property and possessions and divide them among all according to each one's need. Every day they devoted themselves to meeting together in the temple area and to breaking bread in their homes. They ate their meals with exultation and sincerity of heart, praising God and enjoying favor with all the people. And every day the Lord added to their number those who were being saved. (Acts 2:42–47)

Two thousand years have come and gone since that miraculous Sunday. In the twentieth century, some evangelical and mainline Protestant churches have developed cherished traditions to mark special outpourings of the Holy Spirit during their day. A modern pentecostal movement was born out of several of them, and much good has come of it. Meanwhile, the Second Vatican Council in the Catholic Church began with a prayer for a "new pentecost." In Catholic and Orthodox circles pentecostal movements also began, sometimes with the help of early pioneers from other Christian communities, a sure sign of authentic ecumenical brotherhood and sisterhood. That unity alone represented one of the great evidences of the Holy Spirit's presence.

Unfortunately, there were also small groups and individuals who began to lay some claim on the experience of these encounters with the Holy Spirit, and on the criteria for judging their legitimacy. Tragically, because of abuse, misuse, and selfish ambition on the part of some, the work of the Holy Spirit in our contemporary world has become a point of contention rather than a reason for unity among Christians.

> TRAGICALLY, BECAUSE OF ABUSE, MISUSE, AND SELFISH AMBITION ON THE PART OF SOME, THE WORK OF THE HOLY SPIRIT IN OUR CONTEMPORARY WORLD HAS BECOME A POINT OF CONTENTION RATHER THAN A REASON FOR UNITY AMONG CHRISTIANS.

Was this encounter with the Holy Spirit in the Upper Room, recorded by the apostle Luke in the Acts of the Apostles, really about a show of some kind of power? Was it intended to draw attention to any individual, any cluster of seekers? No. Pentecost equipped all the followers of the Messiah, who had been raised from the dead and ascended to the Father, to become His family on earth. As His Church, we are all called upon and equipped to carry forward His redemptive mission until He comes again.

With that in mind, let us pray that as the family of God— called to follow Him and empowered to serve Him—we will demonstrate a light-filled, joyous Christian faith to an ever-darkening, terrified world.

May our pentecostal experience bring us together as one unified body in Christ, loving one another as He has loved us.

May the Holy Spirit use us to restore the beauty of the Church in our day so that, as God's sons and daughters, we can carry on His continuing mission.

May we find a way to move beyond ourselves and embrace earth-weary souls who so desperately need to catch a glimpse of heaven.

As the Venerable Bede wrote hundreds of years ago,

> A person who trusts that he can find rest in the delights and abundance of earthly things is deceiving himself. By the frequent disorders of the world, and at last by its end, such a one is proven convincingly to have laid the foundation of his tranquility on the sand. But all those who have been breathed upon by the Holy Spirit, and have taken upon themselves by the very pleasant yoke of the Lord's love, and following his example, learned to be gentle and humble of heart, enjoy even in the present some image of the future tranquility.

With this in mind, let us sit humbly with our brothers and sisters—our heavenly family—and await the charisma, the promise, and the mysteries of pentecost that Jesus may have for us today.

And, in this final chapter of her story, let us return one last time to our contemplation of Mary. Was her humility lost when she was again overshadowed and empowered when the Spirit was poured out in the Upper Room? Did she become assertive, haughty, or somehow more self-actualized? There is no reason to think that she suddenly stood up and announced that she, the mother of God, was now a very powerful woman. She did not ask for a special seat in the front of the room. She didn't remind everyone there that she had borne a child through the power of the Holy Spirit, and was therefore His favorite. No, Mary well understood the workings of the Holy Spirit. In fact, she lived in the Spirit. She bore the fruit of surrendered love.

Are we humble, obedient, and faithful enough to take Mary's Way in this too?

A wonderful Eastern father wrote, "The goal of the Christian life is the acquisition of the Holy Spirit." Let us join with him, and with an ancient Western prayer that still echoes in the Church today:

> Come, Holy Spirit, fill the hearts of your faithful and kindle in them the fire of your love. Send forth your Spirit and they shall be created. And You shall renew the face of the earth. O, God, who by the light of the Holy Spirit, did instruct the hearts of the faithful, grant that by the same Holy Spirit we may be truly wise and ever enjoy His consolations, Through Christ Our Lord, amen.

LIVING THE
SURRENDERED LIFE

Whoever loves me will keep my word, and my Father will love him, and we will come to him and make our dwelling with him.
—Jesus, St. John's Gospel 14:23

Jesus, in whom the fullness of God dwells, has become our home by making His home in us. He allows us to make our home in Him. By entering into the intimacy of our innermost self, He offers us the opportunity to enter into His own intimacy with God. By choosing us as His preferred dwelling place, He invites us to choose Him as our preferred dwelling place. This is the mystery of the incarnation. Here we come to see what discipline in the spiritual life means. It means a gradual process of coming home to where we belong and listening there to the voice that desires our attention. Home is the place where that first Love dwells and speaks gently to us. Prayer is the most concrete way to make our home in God.

—Henri Nouwen, Lifesigns, 37-39

For centuries, Christians and other people of faith and goodwill have reflected on a young Jewish woman named Mary. Her *Fiat*, her yes to the invitation of the messenger of God, forever changed the course of human history. It is meant to change our own history by revealing a pattern of living, a way of prayer, and a lifestyle of surrendered love.

Mary stands as both message and messenger. The *Prayer of Mary* is offered as a bridge to heal the factions within the family of the Church, the body of her Son, our Lord and Savior Jesus Christ. The purpose of this book is to focus not so much on devotion *to* Mary as much as the devotion *of* Mary.

Some contemporary books on prayer, spirituality, and faith attempt to reduce the "spiritual" life to a formula that will make us feel better or perhaps help us *achieve* something. In these attempts, they fail to satisfy the hunger of the heart and miss the inner truth of the call to communion with the living God, the very heart of authentic prayer. They also fail to open up the true beauty of the spiritual vocation—the call to live our lives in loving surrender, to God and in God, for others.

Prayer is the doorway into a relationship of intimacy with the God of the whole universe who not only created the world— and all who dwell within it—but who fashioned men and women for communion with Him. In and through His Son, Jesus Christ, we are invited to be re-created, made new, refashioned and redeemed. This is made possible through the great *kenosis*, or self-emptying, of Jesus Christ (Phil. 2:5-7). God, who creates and re-creates us out of love, desires to come and make His home within those who make a place for Him (John 14:23). That "making a place," and the dialogue that it entails, is the heart of prayer.

The Christian revelation answers the existential questions that plague every human heart. The gospel, the "good news" of Jesus Christ, presents the path back to a full communion with God. This path is paved by the exercise of our freedom, by living the surrendered life. We are invited to empty ourselves in order to be filled with His presence. He is the God who comes. Our lives, lived now in God through Christ, proceed through prayer. Prayer becomes the classroom of communion where we can learn and discern the truth about who we are—and who we can become—in Jesus.

In prayer, we begin to understand the reason this communion seems so elusive at times. We begin to see why we feel so lost in an apparent struggle with our own disordered appetites and at odds with the beauty and order of the very creation in which we dwell. That is because prayer opens us up to revelation. True theological insight must be experienced and apprehended through communion with God. That is why the true theologians are mystics.

It is the Christian revelation that helps to explain the seemingly aimless plight of humanity—wandering like Cain in the land of Nod, east of Eden. It tells us that our communion with God was fractured by what Christians call *sin.* Christians of the East, Catholic and Orthodox, speak of the same reality, but often in a different language. They explain the rupture between God and man from a different aspect of the very same truth. The incarnation of Jesus Christ is seen as an aspect of reciprocity. God gives Himself fully to us in Jesus Christ, and in Him we are enabled to give ourselves back. In and through our participation in Jesus Christ, we become, in the words of the apostle Peter, "partakers of the divine nature" (2 Peter 1:4 NKJV). We participate in the communion of trinitarian love.

"Mortal sin is a radical possibility of human freedom, as is love itself," explains the Catechism of the Catholic Church (CCC, Par. 1861). The right exercise of our freedom is a lifestyle of response to continual invitations to communion with God. The spiritual life is all about a renewed commitment through overcoming sin and being made new in Christ, to freely choose God. At its very core, sin is a choice against God's invitation to this communion of love.

God invites; we respond. It is faith that orients and makes it all possible. It also opens up the dynamic life of grace. Living by faith is the beginning of the surrendered life. This is the path to both finding and fulfilling our own vocation. This communion with God is initiated by Him. It is a gift of love, for love can only be accepted through a free response of love. Our response is to flow freely from a heart beating in surrendered love.

The God who is love hungers for the communion of sons and daughters, not the slavish response of those coerced. We hunger for communion with Him because He made us this way. Nothing else will satisfy that deep hunger. The early church father Origen wrote: "Every spiritual being is, by nature, a temple of God, created to receive into itself the glory of God." Classical theology teaches that we are the *image* of God, called into His very inner life through His Son, Jesus Christ.

Through prayer, we recover the capacity for deepening this communion of love, and we plunge ourselves into its embrace. This dynamic way of life makes us new creations. It is an exchange of Love for love. We now cry out with Jesus Christ, "Abba, Father." No longer alienated, we participate in the life of the Trinity. We experience an actual participation in the inner life of God. He dwells in us, and we dwell in Him, through His Spirit. This is the heart of what prayer is really all about. It is not about doing or getting but rather about being, receiving, giving, and loving.

We will live the way we love, and we will love the way we pray.

Prayer helps us to repair the breach and heal the wounds occasioned by our own sin, our choices against God's loving invitations. It reopens the door to new life through Jesus Christ and in Him to communion with the Father, with one another, and with the world He created and is re-creating in Christ. All of this unfolds through the action of the Holy Spirit who leads us into to the very inner life of the Trinity.

This relationship of communion, this lifestyle of prayer, begins as we speak our surrender in the soul, by giving our own fiat. The hunger of the human heart will only be satisfied when we live in God. In this life, we only begin the journey. In the life to come, we will finally experience the fullness of its beauty.

Mary understood. She was a woman totally and completely in love—with God. Mary was a woman of prayer, living in an ongoing conversation and intimate communion with God. We are invited into her prayer, into that same relationship with God. Understanding and living the prayer of Mary is about living a life of surrendered love. It is about *being* more than about doing. It is about response more than initiation. It is about encountering God relationally, personally, and intimately.

Mary's *Fiat,* "may it be done to me according to your word" (Luke 1:38), provides a pattern of prayer and a way to live. As we have seen, her *Fiat* issued forth into praise. This praise became a lifestyle of openness to God. The *Magnificat* begins with the words "My soul doth magnify the Lord" (Luke 1:46-55 KJV), and contains the essence of the Christian life—He must increase, to be magnified, while we decrease (John 3:30). For those with eyes to see, it reveals the meaning of human existence. We were made to give ourselves away in love. The *Fiat* and the entire *Magnificat* constitute a lesson book, a guide to follow for every Christian.

Our daily life, so very real and human, with all of its blessings and all of its pain, is also packed with meaning, purpose, and destiny—if we have the eyes to see, ears to hear, and hearts to respond with the voluntary surrender that was so beautifully expressed by Mary, the Virgin of Nazareth. Her response reveals a heart of faith. This lesson book is desperately needed in an age so characterized by pride, arrogance of power, and grandiosity. Mary's entire life shows us what our own lives can become if we follow a trajectory of surrendered love.

Mary said yes to the invitation to love and humbled herself. She confronted her own fears and entered into a new way of living. Her simple response overflowed into her *Magnificat* of praise. Through this response, she assumed a life posture of receiving and giving and became a fruitful woman, a "God-bearer" or "Mother of God" (which are both translations of the Greek *Theotokos*). She brought forth the Word of God and "the Word became flesh and dwelt among us" (John 1:14 NKJV).

Her humble surrender bore the fruit of her *Magnificat,* which bore the fruit of the Word, both spoken and birthed through her. This is the trajectory of every Christian's life, the prototype of the vocation of every human person who chooses to say yes to God. We were made to live the surrendered life.

God is not an add-on to our lives. Rather, He is the source and the summit. Authentic spirituality is "inside out" rather than "outside in." God comes and lives within us, and we find our home in Him. There is a way, a pattern, which all men and women are invited into—not just once, but daily. In this way, Mary's life revealed the deeper meaning of every human life. It showed us a path to what Christian Scripture calls the "more excellent way" (1 Cor. 12:31), the way of love.

Mary walked this way with the beauty borne of humility.

Is it any wonder that the early Christians painted her image in the catacombs during their moments of fear, persecution, and doubt? They found great inspiration from this little woman of great faith. In her yes, they came to understand that ordinary people can change human history. They were inspired to add their own yes, their own fiat, to hers.

Is it any wonder that the writings of the early fathers of the Christian Church were also replete with reflections on this woman who said so few words in the biblical text? That is because it is not about an abundance of our words, but rather about our receptivity to the Word.

Justin Martyr, and many other early Christian apologists, found in Mary's obedient yes to the angel, the undoing of the "no, I will not serve" uttered in rebellion by the first woman, Eve. They called Mary "the Second Eve," the mother of a new creation, because she said yes and in her womb carried the one whom the Christian Scriptures call the "last Adam" (1 Cor. 15:45). Jesus Christ was born from her as the firstborn of a new race of men and women who would themselves come to find a new birth through His life, death, and resurrection.

That same Redeemer now desires to reside within and live through all of those who choose daily to respond to the invitation of love, like Mary did—all who choose to live the surrendered life.

Mary's choice, her response to the invitation of a God who respects human freedom, is a singularly extraordinary event in all of human history. However, it is meant to be much more. It is an invitation to each one of us to explore our own personal histories and to write them anew in Him.

Let us pray the Prayer of Mary.

Drowsy in the hot Ephesus sun,
I stare at my wrinkled hands
And I remember.

First the emptiness:
Yes, they told me he was back,
Yes, I saw him for myself,
But my heart remained cold, strangely detached.
Even as he vanished into the clouds, I was unmoved.
Enough goodbyes, I told myself,
A little sad,
And somehow relieved.

Later, I was praying with his friends
When a fresh wind wafted among us.
Crowned with tiny flames,
We stared at one another, laughing in amazement.
Meanwhile flickering in my darkness.
A spark ignited, filling me with fire,
With broken bread,
With another warm deep drink of Cana's wine.

Once again he stirred within me,
A greeting from a friend,
Alive again. Both he and I.

—*Lela Gilbert*

To Pope John Paul II, who became the prophetic word that he spoke to the Church and the world, having been poured out, through his suffering and weakness as a drink offering, in surrendered love to the Lord. He taught us how to live, love, suffer, and die for the Lord.

To my dear wife and best friend, Laurine, who has shown me through all these years together the beauty and dignity of the "feminine genius" by living the "Fiat" in her holy vocation as wife, mother, sister, and model.

To Father Philip Bebie, priest and servant of God, who through his life, suffering, and death taught me the way of Mary.

To the humble Virgin of Nazareth, whose openness and surrender to God's invitation changed the world. All generations have indeed called you "blessed," and I am numbered among them.

Totus Tuus!

ABOUT THE AUTHORS

REV. MR. KEITH FOURNIER is a deacon in the Roman Catholic Church and serves the Melkite Greek (Byzantine) Catholic Church (with approbation). He is a lawyer, author, scholar, broadcaster, activist, and academic. He holds a bachelor's degree in Philosophy and Theology (summa cum laude) from Franciscan University of Steubenville, a master's degree in Sacred Theology from the John Paul II Institute of the Lateran University (magna cum laude), and a Juris Doctor from the University of Pittsburgh School of Law. He is the founder of Common Good, an open movement of Christians building a culture of life, family, freedom, and solidarity. Fournier has written seven books, numerous booklets, and hundreds of articles on issues related to faith, family, evangelization, and Christian unity and spirituality.

LELA GILBERT is a Gold Medallion-winning freelance writer/editor of forty books for houses such as Tyndale, W Publishing Group, Multnomah, and Baker.